With Good
Reason

To Marjie

Contents

7

*I*ntroit

"Give Me One Good Reason"

*G*ive me one good reason for believing in God, Doc. . . . Just one."

He was a good-looking, intense student. His whole posture registered the earnestness of his inquiry. "Just one," he urged.

Seated on the teacher's desk, I began to formulate some of the traditional arguments for the existence of God. But he gave me no opportunity to launch them.

"I mean, just look at the world," he rushed on. "It's full of pain from top to bottom. One animal survives by living off another. And as for man, the agony of human existence is more than you can imagine. If God is responsible for this kind of world, I don't want anything to do with him."

Which of the classic arguments for the reality of God would you appeal to in this instance? Clearly, rational statements would not touch this man's real questions. His feelings were deeply involved.

All I could say was, "Man, you're hurting, aren't you?"

When he admitted he was, I added, "Well, you surely can see that no amount of intellectual discussion will really get at your hurt. We must start our reply from a different point." And I tried to put his inquiry into a different perspective.

But my reply turned out to be not so much argument as affirmation. And most doubters—no matter how much they hurt—tend to be skeptical about confessions of faith.

Quite different was the simple, poised confidence of the cultured professor and his wife. "Religion is all right for those who need it," they said. "We just don't need it."

And apparently they didn't. No agony here—at least none that showed. No heartfelt questions here. Only coolly reasoned assurance. At least that's what it looked like. So I could only nod polite acceptance.

"In the ten years I've been out of college, the question whether God exists just hasn't been important to me."

The quiet statement was made by a young married man. Active church member. Lovely wife and family. Promising career. Children in Sunday school, of course. In fact, he himself had taught a class.

But whether God really exists hadn't been particularly important to him. When the preacher talked about God, this young man turned off his listening device—turned it on again if the subject ever veered around to "practical" matters.

And now . . . well, the subject was open somehow. At least he was willing to inquire.

And the cute coed. "But what do you *hear?* I mean, when you pray, do you hear a voice?"

"Of course not," I replied—as if the question was just a little silly.

But she persisted. "What do you hear?"

Sobered, I had to admit that what I hear is silence. Ideas. Things I've learned here and there. Hopefully adding up to "divine" guidance.

"And this is God?"

How does one address himself to this many-sided search for God? Or to the disinterest in searching?

Simply to outline a reasonable faith will certainly leave deeper agonies untouched. (I have tried to deal with these in an earlier discussion.[1]) But such a reasoned approach may be relevant to some of the peculiar issues of our day.

[1] *Even So . . . Believe* (Abingdon, 1966).

In a recent letter a wise friend referred to an observation made by Albert Schweitzer to the effect that one of the greatest needs of our time is "a profound rationalism." Some of us were rather doubtful about this a few years ago. But generations have a way of stirring up their own problems. And Schweitzer's comment seems to have special relevance today.

In any case, what follows is one man's effort to look carefully at the faith in which he already stands. But we all have to stand somewhere. And if our standpoint determines our perspective, it need not spoil our view.

This is one man's attempt to talk in an orderly fashion about the God to whom he has already pledged allegiance. If the allegiance shapes the thought and the language, it need not invalidate either the reasoned argument or the images chosen as pointers to the reality in and beyond the pledged faith.

At least, the effort must be made.

"Give me one good reason. . . ."

P.S. At the conclusion of some of the chapters you will find informal reflections upon the theme just examined. I have called them "exercises" or "songs" or "a reflection."

Someone may ask why they are there.

I can only reply, "Just for fun."

I had fun putting them together, and thought you might enjoy them.

1

May God Be Dead?

Belief in the reality of God has certainly become one of the key issues of our time. Is it possible any longer for an intelligent person to believe in God? Or if we do believe, what do we mean by the word "God"? These are earnest, even desperate questions. The nonreligious answer has always been clear enough. But today theologians, whose business it is to interpret religious faith, speak of the silence of God, the absence, the hiddenness, the eclipse . . . even the death of God. If we want to believe intelligently, or at least think carefully, we should try to understand what these men are saying.

On every side we are being told that it is more and more difficult for modern man to find any real meaning in the word "God." According to one of our ablest young theologians, the word itself has become "a virtually useless vocable today." [1] A sensitive Roman

---

[1] Harvey Cox, *The Secular City* (Macmillan, 1965), p. 244.

Catholic philosopher says plainly, "The man in tune with our culture does not believe in God." [2]

We may accept such judgments as being generally true, and yet ask the specific question, "For whom is it true?" The intellectual? The "average man"? The student? The unskilled laborer? The housewife? The church member? The agnostic? Who is this "modern man" who is having such difficulty with his faith?

Certainly it cannot be true of all these people in quite the same way. So rather than accepting uncritically what is popularly affirmed as fact, we should try to make some distinctions among ways in which and people for whom God may be dead.

There is a beautiful phrase out of the history of religious thought which describes one type of disbeliever—the "cultured despisers" of religion. We all know this sort of untroubled indifference to the claims of belief. But the interesting fact is that this descriptive phrase was first used by a German theologian in the year 1799.[3] So there can't be anything exclusively contemporary about that.

"Secular man" is the phrase currently used. Secular man can no longer believe in God, we are told. But in this context the word "secular" means "not particularly concerned about God." Therefore all that is being

[2] Michael Novak, *Belief and Unbelief* (Macmillan, 1965), p. 41.

[3] Friedrich Schleiermacher, *On Religion: Speeches to its Cultured Despisers.*

14

said is that the man who is not concerned about God cannot believe in God. This is hardly a world-shaking observation, even when it is added that most of our contemporaries fall in this category.

I am not trying to discredit statements about the difficulty of faith—I want simply to understand them. If we are asked to use critical discrimination in relation to religious beliefs, we ought to apply that same discrimination to the general statements which are frequently made about our particular age. Doing this, we must ask, "What do you mean when you say that modern man cannot believe in God? Who is this 'modern man'? And in what ways does he find it difficult to believe?"

Perhaps it would help if we took a look at the historical process by which we have come to this age of unbelief, and the varieties of doubt which are discernible.

THE EMERGENCE OF SECULAR MAN

First we may note that there is an *intellectual secularism*. One root of this is a philosophical tradition going back several centuries[4]—perhaps even to Lucretius, a Roman thinker who wrote his definitive work in the first century before Christ.

[4] In *Religion and the Rise of Scepticism* (Harcourt, 1960), Franklin Baumer speaks of "the development of a powerful sceptical tradition over four centuries and more" (p. 4).

It was Nietzsche's dramatic announcement of the death of God, however, which set the stage for our modern development. This announcement was first made in 1882.[5] And since this was a century after the addresses to the "cultured despisers" of religion, it is clear that Nietzsche was not announcing a new idea, but dramatizing a view already well established.

There is a perceptive insight mentioned by Martin Buber in a footnote which might too easily be overlooked. Buber, crediting Heidegger, refers back to Pascal's phrase, "the lost God" (Pascal died in 1662); then to Hegel's observation, "God himself is dead" (1802); and on to Nietzsche's declaration, "God is dead" (1882). Buber wisely observes that "these three expressions actually mark three very different stages on one road." [6] That the same road is being pursued still further is indicated in his more extended discussion of Heidegger and Sartre. The point to be noted is that it is a long road, and our culture has been moving down it for a long time.

It is also interesting to observe that when Nietzsche's madman made his dramatic pronouncement, he added that the world was not quite ready for this news. " 'I

[5] In *The Gay Science,* and later (1891), in *Thus Spoke Zarathustra.*

[6] *Eclipse of God* (Harper, 1957), p. 31. A similar line of descent, reaching back to a Lutheran chorale and including references to Christian mystics, is given in Henri de Lubac's *The Drama of Atheist Humanism* (Peter Smith, 1964), p. 20.

come too early,' he said then; 'my time has not come yet. This tremendous event is still on its way, still wandering—it has not yet reached the ears of man.' "

There are some who believe that we are living in the time when the full force of this truth is being felt by modern man, certainly by modern intellectual man. The process is neatly stated by Arthur Koestler:

Since the end of the eighteenth century, the place of God has been vacant in our civilization; but during the ensuing century and a half so many exciting things were happening that people were not aware of it. Now, however, after the shattering catastrophes which have brought the Age of Reason and Progress to a close, the void has made itself felt. The epoch in which I grew up was an age of disillusions and an age of longing.[7]

A second root of intellectual secularism is found in the scientific world view which necessarily and properly shapes our thinking about the world. The almost unimaginable distances of outer space; our understanding of the movements of planets, including our own; the discovery of innumerable "worlds" out in these far reaches—all this has effectively destroyed the old snug, three-storied universe of prescientific days. So it becomes hard to think of God as being "up there" or

[7] *Arrow in the Blue* (Macmillan, 1952), p. 52.

"out there," when we are not sure which way is "up," and where "out" may be.

Closely related to these difficulties implicit in scientific thought are the developments of technological knowledge. For science has not remained "pure." It has rushed on to devise an abundance of technological skills that have enabled man to do almost anything—hurl men into space, perform intricate computations at incredible speeds, penetrate the atom itself to release the energy which is imprisoned there.

The implication of such developments is that we no longer need God as an explanation for reality nor as an aid to our limitations. Man is now capable of doing what he used to think only God could do.

Interestingly enough, the man who expresses this point of view most pertinently—for Christians, at least—is Dietrich Bonhoeffer. This brilliant young German theologian joined the conspiracy against Hitler and lost his life as a consequence. His writings, usually fragmentary and unfinished, have been greatly influential during the years since the war.

In his letters from prison, Bonhoeffer wrote: "Man has learned to cope with all questions of importance without recourse to God as a working hypothesis." [8] Later he repeated his estimate of the contemporary situation: "There is no longer any need for God as a

[8] *Prisoner for God* (Macmillan, 1953), Letter of June 8, 1944.

working hypothesis, whether in morals, politics or science. Nor is there any need for such a God in religion or philosophy." [9]

The clue here is the phrase "a working hypothesis," that is, God thought of as the explanation for what we cannot otherwise explain. Clearly, as our scientific knowledge and technical skills develop, we have less need to resort to a "religious" explanation for facts and happenings.

I want to give this argument its full weight and not cut it off before it is measured. But I cannot refrain from saying that the God of intelligent faith has never been appealed to simply as the explanation for what we cannot explain by reference to science or philosophy —at least not in modern times. He is appealed to as the ground of the entire process which we are exploring and about which we are learning. God is not the supporter of our ignorance; he is the source of our knowledge. He is not the answer to problems we cannot solve by ourselves; he poses the problems. [10]

This is to run ahead of the discussion. But we ought to point out such distinctions as we go along.

-•-

Another sort of current unbelief might be called the *practical secularism* of the typical modern man. This

[9] *Ibid.*, Letter of July 16, 1944.
[10] Cf. Novak, *Belief and Unbelief:* "He is the one who makes inquiry itself intelligible" (p. 125).

grows easily out of our admitted technological achievements. It results in an unthinking, taken-for-granted reliance on our own powers rather than a sense of dependence upon God. Increasing numbers of men and women live as if God were dead or as if his reality were a matter of indifference.

If there are floods, we do not blame God for them; neither do we pray to him to stop them. We analyze the factors that have gone into the condition and establish better means of flood control.

If there is poverty in our affluent society, we do not say this is a divinely ordained curse, nor do we pray for deliverance. We establish programs for minimizing these conditions and set aside funds to implement the programs.

Illness and disease are not expected to disappear as a consequence of prayer. We spend millions of dollars in research and come up with vaccines or public health programs or surgical procedures.

Recently I read an article about the typical problems of a middle-aged executive who finds himself disturbed by emotional and vocational problems. He is about as far as he can go vocationally—and he may be anxious about this. His family life may be disturbed by the confusions and frustrations of middle-aged bodies and worn-out marriage relations. He is up against it.

Where is he advised to turn? To God? Certainly not.

To his doctor, who may refer him to a psychiatrist. And to a gym instructor. He isn't advised to fall on his knees in prayer, but to go to the gym for his knee bends. As a matter of practical fact, the word "gym" means more to this man than the word "God."

Some perceptive thinkers will say that the god who is being "murdered" by this kind of technological development is the god of popular religion. The god to whom we turn only when we are in a jam. The miracle worker. The man upstairs. The one up there who likes me. And, these thinkers will add, this god is a false god. We are well rid of him. Most of our creative young theologians embrace this sort of secularization gladly and with enthusiasm.[11]

As we suggested earlier, it is such a god whose irrelevance Bonhoeffer affirms. God as "stopgap." God as "*deus ex machina*." [12] On his own terms, of course, Bonhoeffer is right. We can accept and even be glad for the passing of this particular idol. But we can ask whether this really settles the issue concerning the reality of God.

Certainly for many it does. And this condition is beautifully expressed by a sensitive novelist—not without a mixture of bravado, melancholy, and pathos. He has his protagonist write the following credo:

---

[11] E.g., Harvey Cox, *The Secular City;* Gibson Winter, *The New Creation as Metropolis* (Macmillan, 1963).

[12] Cf. *Prisoner for God,* letters of May 25 and June 30, 1944.

I believe that man must learn to live without those consolations called religious, which his own intelligence must by now have told him belong to the childhood of the race. Philosophy can really give us nothing permanent to believe either; it is too rich in answers, each canceling out the rest. The quest for Meaning is foredoomed. Human life "means" nothing. But that is not to say that it is not worth living. . . . Man has only his own two feet to stand on, his own human trinity to see him through: Reason, Courage and Grace. And the first plus the second equals the third.[13]

·•·

There is one more point on this road from Nietzsche to now—and it may be the most "way out" point of all. Today apparently Christian thinkers are talking about the death of God as an item of faith. The possibility of a *Christian atheism* is being seriously affirmed —first in Germany and now in the United States.

The German phase of this development need be noted only as a matter of history and curiosity. This most recent theological notion—like so many of its predecessors—had its origins in Germany. So when its American sponsors present it as a particularly American product, we should note—as a matter of historical accuracy— that it had its first experimental beginnings in Germany.[14]

[13] Peter De Vries, *The Blood of the Lamb* (Little, Brown, 1961).
[14] See Helmut Gollwitzer, *The Existence of God as Confessed*

In the United States this point of view has been catapulted into prominence by a burst of journalistic attention. Its proponents have styled themselves "radical theologians." And their basic claim is that Christian faith in this secular age must begin by accepting the full secular affirmation of the death of God. In the context of secular thought this may be interpreted to mean that there never was a God. In the context of the declared Christian thought of these men, the phrase means just what it says: Once upon a time there was a God, but he has died.[15]

Since this is a directly theological point of view and professedly Christian, it should not be discussed at this point in our inquiry. That may be relevant later. But in any rehearsal of the varieties of secularism in our time, this most recent development must be noted.

This, then, is where we are. And it should be useful

---

by Faith (Westminster, 1965), particularly his discussion of "The Problem Today," pp. 81 ff. It is Gollwitzer's turgid, plodding study which helped me to see the movement from "nonobjective language" about God, to God as subjective experience only, to the strained efforts at "Christian atheism."

Paul Van Buren, in *The Secular Meaning of the Gospel* (Macmillan, 1963), takes a slightly different route to a rather similar destination. He accepts the thesis that God-language is nonobjective, then rightly sees that linguistic analysis demolishes such language. The end result is his own brand of nontheistic admiration of Christ.

[15] See *Radical Theology and the Death of God* by T. J. J. Altizer and William Hamilton (Bobbs-Merrill, 1966), and *The Gospel of Christian Atheism,* by T. J. J. Altizer (Westminster, 1966).

to see how we have arrived here. Hopefully, we will agree that there is no need to panic. It may be helpful to suggest that Christian thinkers have not been unaware of what has been going on for two centuries. They have sought to address themselves to these developments in many and varied ways. Perhaps we can learn from them, as well as from our contemporaries, how best to engage in conversation with secular men.

CONVERSATION WITH SECULAR MAN

Now that we are here, what can we say? How do we speak about God to the secular man? This is the tough question faced by conscientious believers.

Frankly, I am ready to admit that for a time there may not be anything we can really say to secular man. As long as he is consistently secular he's not going to listen to talk about God. So when he insists that God is dead, it may be that all we can say is, "Are you sure?" And perhaps we should simply admit that until he is ready to open up this question, we can't talk seriously about the possibility of faith.

Maybe he will let us say, "We think the report of God's death is somewhat exaggerated. He isn't really dead. It's just that he isn't showing off to attract your attention. In fact, if you'd give him half a chance, he'd slip in and grab you when you're least expecting it. Maybe that's why you're so intense about this. Why don't you relax and give him a chance? He may surprise you."

Maybe we've said too much already. Perhaps we should just refrain from talking about God until the conversation veers in that direction. Then we may get a chance to mention those experiences and events which give out signals that sound like God.

There is a striking question voiced by Bonhoeffer that is relevant here. "How do we speak . . . in secular fashion of God?" [16] My answer is that we don't really. And the best illustration of this is Harvey Cox, who has tried earnestly and brilliantly to do so.[17] He speaks of "God as a Sociological Problem," and of "God as a Political Issue." But in both instances he is not really speaking of God. As Cox himself recognizes, "God is not simply a different way of talking about man." [18] And as long as he is talking sociology and politics he is not talking about God, but about experiences which give off signals that sound to him like "God." (The secularist, of course, will hear no such signal.) It is not until he begins to discuss "A Theological Question" that he really talks about God.

In any case let us suppose that we and our secular friends are ready to listen to one another, not just talk at one another. The conversation is dipping below the

[16] *Prisoner for God,* letter of April 30, 1944.
[17] See *The Secular City,* pp. 241 ff.
[18] *Ibid.,* p. 259.

surface of most polite conversations—as indeed it has already. What do we have to say?

···

I'd like to look a little more closely at modern man's assertion of autonomy. One of the statements I hear as often as any other is that secular man thinks of himself as autonomous, self-sufficient, able to get along on his own. And we are supposed to agree with him.

Again it is Bonhoeffer who expresses this most eloquently. And again it is one of his telling phrases which seems to sum up the whole matter. We are living he says, in "a world which has come of age." [19] Not only secularists, but theologians and preachers have accepted this judgment unquestioningly, and repeat the splendid phrase until it really begins to ring as if it were true.

I venture to raise the question whether it is literally true that our world has come of age; that is, that we have reached a time of maturity in which we are entirely capable of managing our own affairs all by ourselves.

Has anyone noticed the irony of the fact that this claim was most brilliantly expressed by Bonhoeffer at

[19] *Prisoner for God,* letter of June 30, 1944. Bonhoeffer himself may have had some misgivings about this judgment. In his thoughts to the child about to be baptized, he writes, "The world is controlled by forces against which reason is powerless." We must ask, then, how such a world can be said to have come of age.

the very time he was being held prisoner by one of the most demonic tyrannies the world has ever seen? And that this political and military evil put him to death? And not only this young theologian, but countless numbers of his contemporaries. And is this particularly vile offspring of modern man's ingenuity an evidence of our having come of age? Is it possible that our self-announced maturity is denied by our own violent behavior?

I should venture to say that Bonhoeffer's bland salute to our age is sharply countermanded by the brute facts. There is little evidence that men have really come of age or that we have entered into a period of cultural maturity. Technologically we can work miracles. But it is not at all clear that we can manage our technology.

It does not follow that we must appeal to religion or to God in order to make up this deficiency. But it does mean that we may seriously question the claim that our world has come of age. It sounds like a word spoken too soon. It looks like an act of faith which requires testing just like any other favorite belief.

Moreover, this claim to autonomy bothers me. When you come right down to it, where is the person who is really a law unto himself? Solely sufficient unto himself?

When you stop to think about it, every one of us is utterly dependent upon the total reality which supports his existence. There isn't one of us who can exist apart from the support of almost everyone else and everything else. To put it at its simplest level, we owe our lives to our parents and families and beyond them to the society which sustains us. And to the world which furnishes air to breathe and food to eat. And beyond that to the totality of things. . . . How shall I say it? Whatever the total reality of the cosmos may be, you and I are dependent upon it for our very lives.

If you don't really believe it, just think how easily your life may be snuffed out . . . a little shift in body chemistry . . . a too-long hesitation in that patient, pumping heart . . . a blow to a vital part of the body . . . shut out certain elements in the atmosphere and we'd suffocate in a moment . . . and for goodness' sake, don't let anything stop the sun!

The fact is, not a one of us makes his own life. You are, as some philosophers say, "thrown into" existence. Your life is *given* to you. You don't create it, you *receive* it.

For the religious man this becomes a profoundly significant religious fact. And for the secular man to deny it may be simply to repeat the old, old fallacy of Adam.

••

Another consideration which tantalizes me is the possibility that you and I may share in the responsibility for the "absence" or "silence" or "death" of God.

One thing that bothers me in so much talk about the death of God is the absence of serious attention to this possibility. It is assumed that "the death of God" is something which has "happened" in the very structure of reality. One of the most eloquent witnesses to this viewpoint writes, "It is not just that a capacity has dried up within us; we do not take all this as merely a statement about our frail psyches, we take it as a statement about the nature of the world and we try to convince others. God is dead." [20]

Nevertheless, the question must be raised whether we may share responsibility for this crisis in faith. Indeed, when the same man confesses, that the theologian "really doesn't believe in God, or that there is a God, or that God exists," and adds that he "is alienated from the Bible, just as he is alienated from God and the church," [21] the question is not easily put down. It may just be that the silence of God is really an impediment in our hearing. The absence of God may be the other side of our being lost. The death of God may be the death of something within ourselves.

This is why I prefer Buber's luminous phrase, "eclipse of God." First of all, it suggests that our crisis is not an occurrence in "the nature of the world," but

[20] William Hamilton in *Radical Theology and the Death of God*, p. 28.
[21] *Ibid.*, pp. 88, 90.

is a happening between ourselves and this reality. "An eclipse of the sun is something that occurs between the sun and our eyes, not in the sun itself." [22]

Moreover, Buber's phrase suggests that we share in the responsibility for what has happened. Even Nietzsche's madman confessed this: "*We have killed him—* you and I. All of us are his murderers." And Buber's comment about Sartre is exactly relevant to every secular man: "[He] has started from the 'silence' of God without asking himself what part our not hearing and our not having heard has played in that silence." [23]

Exactly. The crucial question is whether we are willing to consider the possibility that there may be something in us, in our condition, which plays a part in our difficulty with faith. Secular man—whether Adam or you or me—resents this implication. But if we are to think honestly, we must face it as a possibility.

••

Adding these two considerations together gives rise to a third, which is different from the sum of the two: whether there may be some basic human need to which only a "religious" answer is adequate. I don't want to push such an argument too hard or too fast, but neither can we push it aside.

First we note that our self-styled autonomy isn't

[22] *Eclipse of God,* p. 34.
[23] *Ibid.,* p. 92.

quite as self-sufficient as we thought. We realize that our existence is dependent upon a lot of factors we can neither cause nor control. We are up against something considerably bigger than we are. Then we admit to a sneaking suspicion that we have had a hand in getting to the place we are currently in. Do these add up to a need for an authentic relation to this totality to which we owe our existence? At least some basic sense of the meaning of it all? And may this need admit of no other than a religious answer?

(By the way, this word "religious" is subject to a variety of uses these days. I'm using it in the common-sense meaning of talk or thought about God, our relationship with something beyond ourselves, consideration of a reality more than human.)

Bonhoeffer dismisses any such argument decisively. But I think he does this too easily. He is dealing with a limited notion of God at these points. He refuses to appeal to God as a problem-solver. This is authentic. But he seems to say there can be no appeal to any inherent religious need in man. And here I think he is mistaken. He rejects the existentialist's appeal to "the so-called ultimate questions" of death and guilt. Here I think he is on debatable ground.[24]

In any case I should be forced to say that if there is not some inherent human need to which faith is the answer, then religion is really irrelevant, and let's forget

[24] *Prisoner for God,* esp. in letters of April 30 and June 8, 1944.

it. Buber presses to this deeper issue: "[The problem] focuses finally in the question of whether the perseverance of the 'religious need' does not indicate something inherent in human existence." [25]

And I would want to press still further. Is not what is inherent in human existence a reflection of the nature of the reality to which we owe our existence? This argument is not an appeal to God as *deus ex machina*. It is to ask a serious question. Is there a profound aspect of our existence which requires an authentic relation to the reality which sustains our existence? And if the answer to this is affirmative, we must ask a further question. Is this "need" simply a confession of weakness, a cause for wishful thinking? Or does it reflect something in the sustaining reality out of which we have emerged?

Not too fast now, demurs the thoughtful secularist. Not too fast. All right, I don't want to push. But can we look at the issues? Can we admit that these may be the key questions? If so, we can talk some more.

[25] *Eclipse of God,* p. 90.

REPRISE

When we come right down to it, we really aren't as self-sufficient as we might like to think. Every last one of us is dependent upon a total reality which is entirely beyond his control. Let's not pretend to be more autonomous than we really are. Let's face the fact of our limitedness.

If we are honest, we admit to a slight suspicion that we—our generation and those that preceded us—have had something to do with our present religious uncertainty. We admit this with respect to social issues and personal behavior. Why not admit it in terms of our religious condition?

There may just possibly be a need rooted in our limitedness-plus-responsibility. This may call for a response or a relationship, the full dimension of which we can only call religious. I mean, more than psychological. More than sociological. When we pursue this need, it seems to draw us to a deeper dimension of thinking and living which begins to look suspiciously like what we call religion.

A Reflection

What must God think
As he hears himself
Politely bowed out of the universe.
Consigned to the limbo of outworn creeds,
Along with fairies and spooks and witches?

Some say he laughs—
("The times of this ignorance God winked
    at")—
Or is it pain that so contorts his face?

How would you like to be asked
To leave the house you built?
To be dismissed from minds you shaped
Laboriously, down endless years?
To be expelled from hearts you loved,
You taught to love, by giving love?

It would be funny . . .
If it were not so ludicrous . . .
If it were not so sad.

2

Is It Reasonable
to Believe?

*W*hich way should the conversation turn? With some hesitancy, I suggest that we consider the reasonableness of faith in God. And to indicate both the relevance and the limitation of this approach let me state the cause for my hesitancy.

Appeal to the reasonableness of faith has been out of fashion in philosophical and theological circles for several generations. Ever since Immanuel Kant demolished the traditional arguments for the existence of God—then someone else demolished Kant's own favorite argument—Christian thinkers, Protestant at least, have put little value on conventional attempts to indicate that there is good reason for believing in God. And, of course, secular philosophy has consistently discounted such arguments.

So I want to make it quite clear that I have no interest in trying to "prove the existence of God." And I want to be equally emphatic that faith in God does not really depend on the persuasiveness of such arguments. The need for this emphasis can be indicated by reference to a statement in a little book which has enjoyed a phenomenal response by the general public, Bishop Robinson's *Honest to God*.

Bishop Robinson begins his discussion of theism with the statement, "Traditional Christian theology has been based upon the proofs for the existence of God." [1] This assertion requires serious qualification. Christian theology has never been based upon any kind of philosophical argument. Its claim has been that God has revealed himself in Christ. This assertion has never been subject to philosophical proof. Such arguments have been used simply to indicate that belief in God—which is part of Christian faith—may be reasonable.

Moreover, though it may be true that "traditional" Christian theology has appealed to such "proofs," it is also true that for several generations Christian thinkers have given little weight to these conventional arguments. Belief in God does not stand or fall with any supposed proof of its validity. Let's recognize at once—and this is no new admission at all—that there is no convincing proof for the reality of God.[2]

Then why bother?

[1] John A. T. Robinson, *Honest to God* (Westminster, 1963), p. 29.
[2] Perhaps it should be acknowledged that some Catholic thinkers

Is It Reasonable to Believe?

First of all, because I think such a concern is still expressed by most inquirers. Outside the highly sophisticated, technical areas of philosophical and theological debate, this issue is still vital. Most of us want to know whether it is reasonable to believe in God.

This gives rise to the second reason for such an approach. Some of us think that the reasonableness of faith ought not to be dismissed so casually. It is too commonly assumed nowadays that the man of reason can go in only one direction—toward unbelief or, at best, agnosticism. Some of us think this is a false assumption. We believe that faith in God is just as reasonable as faith in no-God. Maybe even more so. And we want to state our reasons for believing this, if for no other purpose than to keep alive for the thoughtful inquirer the option of faith in God.

The limitation and allure of such a discussion are beautifully stated by Carl Michalson:

The question about the possibility of God's reality is unanswerable within history. It would be unwise, however, to neglect the innuendo in the fact that the question is so unavoidable. "The heart has reasons the head knows not

---

seem to take a somewhat different approach to this issue. Some believe that the existence of God can be proved by reasonable demonstration, though the character and purpose of God can be known only by revelation.

of." Not to transcribe the reasons of the heart is philosophically irresponsible.[3]

For a whole generation now, a dominant Christian opinion has been that we can only declare our faith on a "take it or leave it" basis. (This is Bonhoeffer's description of the Barthian emphasis.[4]) Such an emphasis may have been necessary and valid at its own moment in history. But like most reactions, it may have swung too far. And it may be that the time has come for us to say things a little differently. At least I am unwilling to surrender the field to those who claim that the only rational position is unbelief, or—as I prefer to call it—belief in no-God.

I believe that faith in God is eminently reasonable. Believers in no-God will not be convinced by my discussion. But at least let it be recognized that for the reasoning inquirer there is a viable alternative to nontheism or agnosticism. Let modern man realize that facts or rational arguments do not compel a secularistic conclusion. What you have to do is make up your mind . . . choose . . . decide.

A CONFESSIONAL APPEAL TO REASON

There are two traditional approaches to the reality of God which have always appealed to me. They are

[3] *The Hinge of History* (Scribner's, 1959), p. 136.
[4] Cf. *Prisoner for God,* letter of May 5, 1944.

not really arguments. They are more like what one man called "persuasions." Asked to speak on the reasonableness of faith, he refused to offer arguments but simply listed several "persuasions" which meant much to him. Incidentally, they bore no resemblance at all to what I am presenting here, which might suggest that each person will find his own persuasions.

There are more sophisticated ways of getting at this issue. But frankly, they are beyond my competence. And just as frankly, I think they are too technical for most of us. So I'd prefer to keep the approach as simple as possible without being false to the facts of our experience.

This, then, is a confessional appeal to reason. I stand in faith—and you have known this from the beginning. In this posture there are certain reasoned aspects of faith which are very persuasive to me. Another person might appeal to entirely different reasons. But these are the thought-provoking considerations which make sense to me.

The first is an updated version of what is known historically as the argument from design or order. The traditional argument has to be modified in the light of newer scientific thought. But the basic insight seems still to be valid.

We live in a world of order. The universe operates

in a dependable manner according to regular procedures. Our existence depends upon this orderliness. We measure our lives by the regular movement of the sun and the satellite on which we live. The stability of a great building and the explosive power of an atomic bomb are possible because of the orderliness of the elements involved. The supersonic speed of jet planes and the stalling of my automobile when it runs out of gas are expressions of the underlying regularities in the nature of things.

The world is orderly. We can count on it. The careful scientist may insist that this regularity is computed in terms of probabilities only. And there may be occasional interruptions of or collisions among events. But our lives depend upon the dependability of natural processes. This fact is so obvious that we tend to take it for granted. But if we stop to think about it, it is a quite remarkable fact.

One recent winter morning I had to fly out of our city on a flight leaving before daybreak. We took off in the cold murky dark of the morning and rose through heavy clouds into the half-light of the upper air. We could see that we were flying directly into what Homer once called "rosy-fingered dawn," viewed from a perspective which the old Greek had never imagined. The beauty was indescribable. The eastern sky grew lighter. The colors changed, casting incredible reflections among the clouds. And suddenly the sun burst over the horizon in a glorious brilliance.

I found myself saying, half in exasperation, half in prayer: My God, this happens every morning. At the very moment when I am reluctantly fighting my way out of the stupor of sleep, already anticipating the round of jobs to be done, this miracle occurs—and I take no note of it. This miracle of order upon which the regularity of our human procedures is utterly dependent . . . this life-giving miracle without which earth would be reduced to a cold, dead, spinning ball . . . this miracle, embellished with such extravagant beauty—for whose benefit? . . . this miracle occurs every morning. So we don't call it a miracle. But just let it miss one morning and we would be finished. Yet we usually pay little attention to it. We fail to read any meaning in it.

May there be meaning here?

After all, the world need not be orderly. One can conceive of a disorderly world in which nothing is dependable. All would be chaos. (Of course, we have to use the processes of orderly thought even to conceive of this possibility.) Such a world might have been, rather than the one we know. There probably would be no one around to investigate it, since our whole existence seems to depend on these regularities. But surely we can say that the world might have been like that rather than as it is.

How does it happen that this orderly world came to be? We can shrug off the question, but it returns. We can retort that such inquiries smack of metaphysics, but they recur. We can say that the world is what it is and that's all there is to it. It has just happened this way purely by chance. This sounds learned until we check it out against our own experience.

The fact is that wherever we find orderly and dependable processes in our daily life, in the realms for which we are responsible, there we find the work of an ordering mind. In our own experience, order never simply happens. It is ordered. It is called into existence by an ordering mind.

Whether it be the car I drive or the spaceship that hurtles hundreds of miles into space while I "speed" all of five miles distance on the earthbound highway— whether it be the car radio that tunes in on the description of this event or the beams which track the spaceship itself—these amazing mechanisms and their astounding feats do not just happen. They are made. The orderliness of their performances is no accident. If left to chance they never would occur.

The trustworthy, reliable operations of our man-made world (our technology) are utterly dependent upon the order imposed by and utilized by the creative, ordering minds of men. Such regular processes, such orderly events, such dependable instruments do not happen by chance. They are called into being and their regularity is maintained by ordering minds.

On what reasonable grounds, then, should we suppose that what is invariably true in our experience is contradicted in the cosmos which supports our experience? Is it not much more reasonable to suppose that the cosmos operates in ways congruous with the discoveries we make and which we learn are dependable? Order as we know it is the expression of an ordering mind. May we not reasonably guess that the same is true in the total reality which sustains and makes possible our experience?

If we may reason from our direct knowledge, order in the universe implies the work of an ordering cosmic mind or purpose. The leap from chaos to cosmos via chance is a leap of credulity with no basis in daily life. One may take this leap if he chooses. But let's not appeal to reason as justification for such an act of faith. The reasonable inference from our experience is that the presence of order and dependability in the universe implies the operation of an ordering principle, purpose, or power. I should say an ordering mind. For what can impress an ordering purpose, exert an ordered power, fulfill a principle of order, except a mind?

Such considerations point in the direction of what religion knows as God.

This way of thinking may seem quite old-fashioned to some of you. So it may be worth mentioning that in more sophisticated forms it is being renewed by some of our younger theologians who are favorably inclined toward what is known as "process philosophy." These men find in the formidable work of Alfred North Whitehead and Charles Hartshorne a stimulating approach to the nature of reality. And both these thinkers speak persuasively of the reasonableness of theistic faith.

Two young men in particular illustrate this interest in process philosophy: John Cobb and Schubert Ogden. In *A Christian Natural Theology*, Cobb expounds Whitehead's philosophy as a possible ally of Christian theism. Whitehead's discussion of the reality of God is "primarily the traditional one from the order of the universe to a ground of order. . . . That there *is* something which we may properly call God is sufficiently indicated by the kind of order that is visible to all." [5]

••

A second aspect of life as we know it has always seemed significant to me.

[5] *A Christian Natural Theology* (Westminster, 1965), pp. 169, 173.

Ogden's volume, *The Reality of God and other Essays* (Harper and Row, 1966), has been published too recently to receive the sort of attention it really deserves. In it Ogden champions the philosophy of Charles Hartshorne as "a way of conceiving God's reality which is able to do justice to modern secularity" (p. 63). He makes an impressive case for his position that the reality of God is the necessary implication of our scientific and moral experience. One can never say, "This case is closed." But the argument is expounded with clarity and conviction.

In the order of things just outlined, man seems to occupy a rather special place. He not only emerges from the total universal process, but he is aware of this process and of his emergence from it. He looks at, examines, tries to understand this process. Indeed he is aware of himself. He studies, examines, tries to understand himself.

This self-awareness includes all the values and activities which we call personal existence. If we can separate the word from its popular connotations, "personality" is the term which designates all that we can identify as the distinctive qualities and activities of men. Man is a person, aware of himself and his reality, willing his own activity, establishing purposes and moving toward their fulfillment, trying to understand himself and the whole context of his life. This is what it means to be human.

This is a distinctive kind of existence, different from the process out of which it emerges. So Dr. William Pollard, a scientist turned theologian, speaks of "the twofold nature of reality." [6] Carl Michalson insists that history and nature are "two structures of reality." [7] Men who follow the lead of process thought are unwilling to make such a distinction, but they nonetheless insist on interpreting the realm of nature

[6] *Chance and Providence* (Scribner's, 1958), chap. 6.
[7] *The Rationality of Faith* (Scribner's, 1963), pp. 24 ff.

in terms of its highest emergent, human experience.[8]

The key question, it seems to me, is how we must think of the process which produces personal reality. Does this "highest" product—at least the highest we know at present—tell us anything about the process? The reasonable answer would seem to be the affirmative. The product, personality, tells us something about the nature of the process which produces it. The process itself must include the personal elements which appear in the product. In the total reality from which man emerges there must be what we can only call personal reality.

We follow such reasoning all the time. The facts which we discern are taken as clues to the reality in which we live. The physicist dissects the atom and discovers an amazing energy. He concludes that the nature of reality must be something like energy. The biologist observes the many kinds of living reality and wisely infers that in the nature of things there is a quality we identify as life. By the same token we observe and we experience personal reality: self-consiousness, self-knowledge, self-direction. Do these tell us something about the nature of the reality which produced them? They must. They tell us that the ultimate nature of reality must be, or must include, the personal.

[8] So Cobb, *A Christian Natural Theology;* see esp. p. 27. Also Ogden, *The Reality of God,* pp. 57 ff.

When my wife brings a chocolate cake to the dinner table, pointedly mentioning that she baked it "from scratch," we have a right to assume that in the universe which produced it (her kitchen) there existed the ingredient chocolate. To think anything else is unreasonable. If chocolate is in the finished product, it had to be part of the process. It does not appear accidentally. And it cannot appear if it does not exist at all. Whatever is in the product is indicative of what is in the process.

So man is cosmic index. Interestingly enough, Rabbi Liebman said this very clearly some years ago in a book which was influential in quite a different direction. "Why exalt the atom as the clue to truth and ignore the mind of man? Why should we not believe that that which is highest in ourselves is a reflection of that which is deepest in the universe?" [9] Why not, indeed? It seems eminently reasonable.

A young philosopher—a sensitive, eloquent Roman Catholic layman—makes the same point.

Believers believe that the human person, though infinitesimal and seemingly insignificant among the galaxies, is the interpretive key to the universe and to the presence and activity of God. . . . Nevertheless, although the human person is humble and puny, he does seem to be the source

[9] Joshua L. Liebman, *Peace of Mind* (Simon and Schuster, 1946), p. 168.

of science and morality, and indeed of the whole project of interpretation. As the source of this project, he also seems to be its key. He interprets; and he is the key to what he interprets.[10]

Human intelligence implies the existence of intelligence in the very nature of things. Human personality implies the existence of personality at the very core of reality. Such language points toward the reality expressed in the word "God."

Now an interesting fact emerges. If we put together the two considerations we have just outlined, we have a basis for supposing there may be some meaning to our existence.

The totality upon which I am dependent is dependable. It need not be, but it is. It is characterized by an order which I may discern and which I discover to be dependable. This regularity makes possible my existence. It supports my freedom, the root of my dignity as a person.

Secondly, the responsibility which I sense, or at least am willing to take upon myself, is the other side of my freedom. This free responsibility is part of being a person. And my existence as a person is not a mere ac-

[10] Michael Novak, *Belief and Unbelief,* pp. 189-90.

cident, not an event alien to reality, but is expressive of the deepest reality which has produced me.

It need not be this way. I could be "an accidental collocation of atoms," [11] with no support in the nature of things. It could be that the entire race of such collocations is destined to be reduced to the mindless whirlings of matter. But there is reason to think otherwise. There is reason to believe that my very reasonableness, my personal existence, is congruous with the ultimate nature of things and is supported by reality.

These two factors make it possible to believe that human existence has meaning. And this is one of the deepest needs of our being. As Camus exclaims, "The meaning of life is the most urgent of questions." [12] We are contending here that a reasonable approach to reality offers an answer to this question. Reality evokes need. Need responds to reality.

Interestingly enough, there is an inclination among some Christian thinkers to interpret the doctrine of creation in terms of meaning. To affirm that reality is contingent upon the creative purpose of God is really to affirm that existence has meaning. So Carl Michalson writes that the doctrine of creation has to do "not with the temporal origin nor with the technical explanation of the universe but with the meaning of man's life."

---

[11] Bertrand Russell's phrase in *A Free Man's Worship.*
[12] Albert Camus in *The Myth of Sisyphus* (Knopf, 1955).

It declares that "man's life does not derive its meaning from the world but from its relationship to God." [13]

Langdon Gilkey argues quite persuasively (at least to a believer) that the intelligibility and meaning of the world are grounded in belief in creation. The whole structure of science, the empirical approach to reality, is made possible by such confident faith.[14]

The relationship between the traditional doctrine of creation and modern belief in the orderliness of the universe has been pointed out many times. A generation ago Whitehead wrote, "The faith in the possibility of science . . . is an unconscious derivative from medieval theology." [15] That is to say, the confidence that natural processes are orderly—so essential to scientific thought —is rooted historically in confidence that a divine Orderer sustains these processes.

In *The Coming World Civilization,* William Ernest Hocking has written with profound eloquence about the philosophical and ethical foundations which must support this future world. Some of these foundations have been shaped in our present civilization and must be reformed for the future. Trust in the dependability of nature, for instance, is the basis for our scientific achievements and must be a persistent aspect of any

[13] *The Rationality of Faith,* pp. 43, 44.

[14] *Maker of Heaven and Earth* (Doubleday, 1965), chaps. 5 and 6; esp. pp. 106-20.

[15] Alfred North Whitehead, *Science and the Modern World* (Macmillan, 1926), p. 18.

future world view. Such trust, he shows, is an outgrowth of the religious faith which is one of the roots of our civilization. "The characteristic development of science in modern Europe is not only a corollary of the religion of Europe but in a significant sense part of that religion." [16] Secularism may disown such parentage. But if a technical and scientific civilization is to endure, these origins may have to be acknowledged and these roots kept alive.

There is an order in reality upon which we are utterly dependent. Is this order in turn dependent upon, expressive of, an Orderer?

Our own free responsibility may be interpreted as no accidental happening but as an emergent expression of the reality which produces us. Is this personal existence which we know indicative of a deeper Personal Reality?

If we can answer these questions positively, we may affirm that the meaning of our life is to relate ourselves to this ordered Personal Reality whose creatures we are.

A Call for Courage

Admittedly, all that we have been able to say thus far falls short of being compelling. It does not prove the validity of belief. We may hope that it points to the reasonableness of believing in God. We may even

[16] *The Coming World Civilization* (Harper, 1956), p. 62.

hope that the total effect of the discussion may be "impressive even if it is not decisive," as one author says of the arguments for the reality of God.[17]

Of course, we have always known that faith is finally a choice among alternatives, that there is never any conclusive proof for a faith. Where we stand is always a decision. Our ultimate conviction is always a commitment. But the choice is not blind. The decision is not unreasoned. The commitment is not arbitrary. Indeed, it may be that our decision is elicited by something decisive in the nature of things.

Recently my church sponsored an exhibition of contemporary art, centering around the theme of life's meaning. On the opening night several of the artists were present and generously offered to answer any questions the people might want to ask. Of course, the inevitable question was flung out, "What does it mean?" "What are you trying to say?"

In reply, one of the young men spoke of the different "language" which the artist uses, the language of color, line, texture. And he challenged us to take the trouble to learn to "read" the artist's language. Then he said a very interesting thing: "The artist has committed himself. Perhaps what is required is a corresponding commitment from the viewer."

Is this the way we must read the universe? Could

[17] Daniel Jenkins, *The Christian Belief in God* (Westminster, 1963), p. 57.

it be that the Artist has committed himself? And that we must correspondingly commit ourselves?

So we have to go beyond reason. Or perhaps we might better say we have to carry reason to a further affirmation. And what is required partakes of the nature of courage. It is Paul Tillich who has spoken most eloquently of the role of courage in understanding ourselves and our world. "There are no valid arguments for the 'existence' of God, but there are acts of courage in which we affirm the power of being, whether we know it or not." [18]

A troubled playwright has one of his characters write a poem which may express the playwright's own prayer.

> How calmly does the orange branch
> Observe the sky begin to blanch
> Without a cry, without a prayer,
> With no betrayal of despair.
>
> O, courage, could you not as well
> Select a second place to dwell,
> Not only in that golden tree
> But in the frightened heart of me? [19]

So we affirm the reasoned right to courageous affirmation.

[18] *The Courage to Be* (Yale University Press, 1952), p. 181.
[19] From Tennessee Williams, *The Night of the Iguana.* © 1961 by Two Rivers Enterprises, Inc. Reprinted by permission of New Directions Publishing Corporation.

REPRISE

The reality upon which we are dependent is itself dependable. It is sometimes deceitful, occasionally destructive, but generally dependable. Indeed, we could not exist if this were not so. There is an orderliness in reality which we may trust. And this order may possibly be understood most fully as the purposive expression of a divine Orderer.

The personal existence which we know most intimately is our own. And it often seems very precarious in an apparently impersonal world. Yet we are the products of this cosmic process. So there ought to be some congruity between the world and ourselves. If we take our own reality with some seriousness, we may accept the universe as "radically personal." [20] We may even say that the ultimate reality can best be identified as Person.

If so, the meaning of our lives may be found in discovering the purposes of this ultimate Person. We dare believe that they are life-affirming, life-supporting. And that our lives are given significance in courageous assent to these purposes.

[20] Michael Novak's phrase, *Belief and Unbelief,* p. 189.

The Three Dares
An Exercise

Once upon a time there were—because always there are—three dares: the big dare, the middle-sized dare, and the little dare. It requires quite some courage to take the big dare. Men who are willing to venture, though perhaps not quite so much, take the middle-sized dare. Men of scant courage espouse the little dare.

The little dare is agnosticism. For some reason, agnosticism has gained status as a rather nervy position. But it requires no courage to say, "I don't know," and let it go at that. The agnostic runs no risk in taking such a position. He hides from all risk behind the facade of not knowing. He acknowledges only "the nothing-deity of agnosticism."

"The agnostic gives up even the search for God":
   J. C. Murray

"Agnosticism is impossible as a policy of life":
   Michael Novak

The middle-sized dare is atheism, the belief in no-God. At least the atheist is willing to stake his life on something. He risks a position, although an uncertain one. He says there is no evidence for God—a statement of limited demonstrability, at best. Therefore, he continues, I do not believe in God. He might better say that he believes in no-God. For what he affirms is a faith, not a proved conclusion. And he is willing to stake out a faith and take a chance that it may be true.

"Atheism is a cruel and long-range affair": Sartre

"Atheism appears as the willingness to assume human responsibility to the full": Lacroix

The big dare is theism. Here a man looks clear-eyed at the fact that there is no proof; there are only "persuasions." He sees poignantly that there are evidences which do not always lend themselves to his faith. Moreover, he senses that if he says "yes" to this faith, he is surrendering to a total claim, responding to an utter demand. And all of this is in his mind when he affirms courageously, "I believe in God." He lets his faith direct his life. He risks all he is on this faith. And judging by the look on his face, courage is met with confirmation.

The Three Dares: An Exercise

"The courage to be is the courage to accept oneself
    as accepted in spite of being unacceptable":
    Tillich

"Who am I? They mock me, these lonely questions of
    mine.
Whoever I am, Thou knowest, O God, I am Thine!":
    Bonhoeffer

Once upon a time . . .
There always are . . .
Three dares . . .
And Everyman must choose.

3

May We Think of
God as Personal?

*D*id you notice that sentence I slipped in just before the end of the previous chapter? I'd be surprised if you didn't—and even more suprised if you didn't challenge it. I ventured to speak of ultimate reality as Person, capital P and all. This must be challenged. No self-respecting secularist will let me get away with this without raising serious questions. Indeed, there are a good many Christian thinkers who are suspicious of such language. Do we really have any right to talk like this?

Well, how else shall we talk? What kinds of images and symbols are available to us when we talk about God? "What language shall I borrow?" is the question not only of piety but of honest thinking.

The problem of language is acknowledged by every serious thinker I read, whether secularist or Christian or hesitant inquirer. The basic difficulty is that language is limited. How can we talk about God in man-made language? Anthropomorphic is the technical term —and often used to indicate disapproval. But man-shaped language is all we have. We must use words, images, symbols which grow out of our own experiences. And God—if he or it is—is more than our human experience. (This, by the way, is being debated currently. But let it pass for the moment.) So the reality of God is always more than we can put into words because we just don't have the words for it.

Let's agree at the outset, then, that in talking about God, *words are pointers only.* They point to a reality beyond themselves, greater than their meaning. "How else can we speak about the transcendent Mystery except by using words that point toward it and then, reminding ourselves of their finite character, try to show where they fail to point." [1] One task of thinking, then, is to choose the pointers which will indicate most and—to the best of our understanding—most accurately.

Among philosophers and theologians there is a great deal of serious debate about language. It frequently gets very technical. I don't dare become involved in its intricacies, but will settle for staking out one or two claims.

The word "God" cannot be just a term to denote

[1] William Hordern, *Speaking of God* (Macmillan, 1964), p. 125.

a particular sort of human experience. If "God" simply means "something that happens to us, in us, under certain circumstances," then why bother with the word at all? Let's settle for a good, solid humanism.

It seems to me that the word "God" must be taken to mean the Reality at which we were pointing in the last chapter. The Ordering Personal Reality, which is ultimate—and the capitals are simply intended to indicate this ultimacy.

The "Wholly Other" is a term—frequently abused—which indicates the ultimate which limits us, which we experience as other than ourselves, and which suggests "God." So Cobb affirms that "all experience of God . . . is experience of one who is 'wholly other.' " [2] And, he adds, both numerically and qualitatively other. Yet "the otherness of God expresses itself, paradoxically if you will, in his absolute nearness." [3] Philosophy may challenge this. But it certainly is what religion is about . . . religion as adoration, as worship, as service.

[2] *A Christian Natural Theology,* p. 238. Cf. Cox, *The Secular City,* p. 262: "Thus we meet God at those places in life where we come up against that which is not pliable and disposable, at those hard edges where we are both stopped and challenged to move ahead. God meets us as the transcendent, at those aspects of our experience which can never be transmuted into extensions of ourselves. He meets us in the wholly other."

[3] *A Christian Natural Theology,* p. 243. Cf. Michalson, *The Hinge of History,* pp. 153-54: "The transcendence of God does not mean God is very far away. . . . The truth is that God is transcendent because he is so very near and not because he is so very far."

It follows, then, that whatever we say about God must be analogical or symbolic. I'm a little uneasy about those adjectives because they may imply different things to different technical scholars. But they are the only words I can think of. What I mean is this. All we can say is "God is like . . ." We can say, "God is more than we have words for, but this is what is most like him . . ." Or we can tell a story (myth) to illustrate a truth about what we take to be acts of God which are beyond exact expression.

Words are pointers. Some of us believe that personal language is the best indicator to use in speaking about God. To speak of God as Person is most exact, most indicative, most revealing.

GOD AS PERSON

Personalistic language about God is used with some difficulty in our time. Is it the scientific world view which makes it so strange to think of God in personal terms? Or the contortions of philosophy, groping its way into meaningful speech? Or the embarrassing sentimentalities of popularized religion, reducing God to an oversized man? For whichever combination of reasons, many persons are hesitant to speak of God as Person.

Bishop Robinson illustrates the problem neatly in *Honest to God*. He doubtless would never have attempted the preceding chapter—and perhaps wisely. He prefers to start "the other way round," as he calls it. His basic affirmation is: "God is, by definition, ultimate reality. And one cannot argue whether ultimate reality exists." [4]

This seems harmless enough—and indeed it is, because it really says nothing. No perceptive secularist will be taken in for a moment. It is nothing but another of the classical arguments for the existence of God smuggled in, using contemporary language. "Existence" is slipped into the definition of "God," and then it just follows that "he is."

No careful doubter will let this go by. To define God as ultimate reality, and then say that ultimate reality must exist, will not persuade any thoughtful person. He will still argue whether God, in any meaningful sense, exists. And despite Robinson's disclaimer, the naturalistic thinker will dismiss not only the so-called supernatural Being of traditional religion, but also the Being itself which the Bishop is seeking to affirm.

But we have to begin somewhere, and having begun at this point, Robinson moves on to speak of God as "the ultimate depth of all our being, the creative ground and meaning of all our existence." And he affirms that "for this way of thinking, to say that

[4] *Honest to God,* p. 29.

'God is personal' is to say that 'reality at its very deepest level is personal.' " [5]

There is a key question to be asked here. What does it mean to say that reality is personal? Does it mean that this reality knows that it exists? Does the ground of our being know that it exists? Does it know that we exist?

If the answers to these questions are negative, we are dealing with a god that doesn't really matter. We can reduce religion to meditation and morality.

If the answers are positive, then we are speaking of God as Person. For this is what personal reality means: self-awareness, self-knowledge, self-direction. To say that God is personal is to say: God knows that he exists (otherwise, we can't really say "he"); he knows that we exist; and this knowledge may be of some concern to him.

Someone, playing on Tillich's familiar phrase "ultimate concern," has suggested that the real question is, "Is the Ultimate concerned?"

Stephen Crane, in a poem written just before the turn of the century, put the issue neatly:

> A man said to the universe:
> "Sir, I exist!"
> "However," replied the universe,

[5] *Ibid.,* pp. 47, 48.

"The fact has not created in me
A sense of obligation."

This is a great divide in our thinking about God. If we say God knows that he exists, we are already speaking of God as Person. Moreover, we may add, he has affirmed certain divine purposes and is working toward their fulfillment. These purposes may involve us, for he knows that we exist. And there is some indication that he even cares about his creation.

···

Reluctance to speak of God as Person is closely related to an even more serious reluctance—usually a downright refusal—to speak of God as *a* Person. This is a rather general attitude among people who think seriously about the reality of God, and is identifiable even among some theologians. For this reason, although I am fearful of getting beyond my depth, I think we must pay serious attention to this issue.

There seem to be two objections to speaking of God as *a* Person.

First, there is the quite proper refusal to consider God as an object "out there" somewhere, among other objects, to be discovered as other objects are. But it seems to me this is a false boogeyman which somebody has erected. To speak of God as a Person does not imply that he is an object, but that he is a Subject . . .

not a thing to be discovered, but a Person to be disclosed . . . not an it, but a Thou.

It seems to me a strange mistake to assume that speaking of God as *a* Being involves us in a subject-object relationship. It does nothing of the kind. It involves us in a subject-Subject relationship, the relation of a person to a Person, or as we have learned to say, an I-Thou relationship.

Much as I hesitate to dispute with Tillich, I can't help but say that I think he is wrong when he argues in this manner. To say that "God as a subject makes me into an object which is nothing more than an object" [6] is just plain false. And someone who knows Tillich's thought better than I will have to tell me why he makes such an error.

To think of—better yet, to encounter—God as Subject is never to destroy the integrity of the human subject who thus meets him. There is evidence that the divine Person wills, above all else, the authentic reality of the human person. There are even those who suggest that the proper existence of man is realized only in personal relation to the living God. Be that as it may, I want to say as clearly as I can that the rather technical dismissal of personal language about God, on the

[6] *The Courage to Be,* p. 185; see also p. 178. I take some courage from the fact that Hordern challenges Tillich's rejection of "person" as a fit symbol for God, on somewhat different terms (*Speaking of God,* pp. 132-34).

supposition that it makes God an "object out there," is simply not valid.

God as a Person is never an object, but always a Subject. He is infinite Person over against us human persons. The relation between us is never I-It. It is always I-Thou, because he can enter into no other relation.

A second objection to personalistic speech about God is that it seems to limit him to human categories, as if we are saying God is a person in the same sense that we are persons. But surely this is to overlook our earlier warning that words are pointers only; and that, especially when we speak of God, we must realize that words are limited and are pointing beyond themselves to a larger meaning.

So when we say that God is a Person, we do not mean that he is limited as we are. Rather he is Person in a sense infinitely beyond our personhood. Our own personal existence is only a pointer to what the existence of God must be. "Man is derivative person, even as God is original Person." [7]

Our personal life is limited, temporal, finite. God is perfect, eternal, infinite Person. And these words are only pointers to the "transcendent," the "wholly other" reality which God is.

Our existence as persons is not only limited, but is

[7] Emil Brunner, *The Divine-Human Encounter* (Westminster, 1943), p. 127; this is a definitive work in relation to what I am trying to say in this section.

also specified by measurable, tangible characteristics: we have bodies, families, addresses, social security numbers. These help to identify us, though they never reveal the real person involved in all those things. God has none of these limitations, which are also identifications. This makes knowledge of him uniquely difficult —about which more later. But it sets his being over against ours. There is a difference. And it may well be an infinite qualitative difference, to use a much-debated phrase from the past. As Barth puts it with a characteristic twist, the question is not whether God is a person, but whether we are.[8]

To affirm that God is a Person, then, is not to delimit his reality. It is to say that this is the best language we can find. So Cobb, following Whitehead's lead (who, by the way, spoke in strikingly personalistic images about whatever God might be)[9] goes beyond his mentor to affirm God as "a living person." [10]

[8] Quoted by Hordern, *Speaking of God,* p. 132. Cf. "We are thinking and speaking only in feeble images and echoes of the person of God when we describe man as a person, as an individual." This is Barth again, as quoted by Gollwitzer in *The Existence of God as Confessed by Faith,* p. 196.

[9] "God is the great companion—the fellow-sufferer who understands" (Whitehead, *Process and Reality* [Harper, 1960], p. 532, quoted by Cobb in *A Christian Natural Theology*).

[10] *A Christian Natural Theology,* pp. 188-92. Ogden, following the lead of process philosopher Hartshorne, argues in a similar manner. "God," he affirms, "is to be conceived in strict analogy with the human self or person." (*The Reality of God,* p. 175; cf. p. 59.)

We admit that the language is limited. But we urge that it is the best we have. To try to find language that goes "beyond" personalistic images usually results in language that is less than personal. As one of our ablest young theologians says, "It is obvious that when men try to find a better way to refer to God than as a person they defeat their purpose. They wish to express God in terms higher than personality, but what they say describes God in less than personal terms." [11] I am convinced that such images as Being or Ground are precisely such less than personal terms.

God is doubtless more than personal. But we cannot say what that "more" is. And we must be careful not to say less. We must use terms which express God's awareness of his own existence, his awareness of and response to our existence, and his will to enter into relations with us. Something of the demand and dilemma is indicated by Donald Baillie.

It is even more important in the modern world to emphasize this truth that God is always and wholly and in every respect *personal*. . . . Personality in God must indeed be a very different thing from personality in us. But that is because we are far from being perfectly personal. God is the only perfectly personal Being.[12]

[11] Hordern in *Speaking of God*, p. 134.
[12] *God Was in Christ* (Faber, 1961), p. 143.

"Within" and Also "Beyond"

There remain a few related considerations to draw together in order to clarify what I am trying to say, and perhaps even to guard it from misinterpretation.

One frequently expressed hesitancy in speaking about God as a Person is that such language easily deteriorates into the sentimental inanities of popular religion. One of the favorite whipping boys of sophisticated thinkers is precisely this pious, oozy sentiment that so often passes for religion. Here God becomes a sort of cosmic pal to whom we turn whenever we need help. The omnipotent good guy who is sure to win in the end. The universal bellhop, eager to deliver a cup of instant success.

If this is caricature, it is painfully close to the truth —and every honest thinker knows it. And some men seem to think that speaking of God as Person runs the risk of sentimentalizing him.

But does a man stop saying to his wife, "I love you," because those words have been bawled by saccharin voices to maudlin lyrics set to shoddy music? They are still the best words—with variations—that we have. And they can be authentic.

By the same token, "God is a Person" are the best words we have. And they can be authentic. It ought to be crystal clear that in the present context they are light years removed from popular sentimentality. They are affirmed as profound truth, honestly reasoned, reverently held. And we know they are pointers, indicating a truth too deep for words.

While we are speaking about dangers—and before we get too far away from the subject—I should like to say that the refusal to speak of God as a Person may betray us into a more sophisticated and more dangerous error: namely, thinking of God and trying to relate ourselves to him as if he were less than personal. This leads to many philosophical and theological notions which may be confusing and corrosive to authentic religious experience. This is one path which has even led to so-called "Christian atheism."

If we have to choose our dangers, I'll run the risk of popular sentimentality. I shall try to guard against it by careful thinking. Still, if popular religion doesn't do anybody much good (as some people say of churchgoing), it won't do much harm either. At least it will do less harm than the negations of much self-consciously sophisticated thought.

But there is a more serious reason for choosing personalistic images of God. They reflect more of Reality. They point to the real depths of Reality. And they touch the springs of our own responsible relation to that Reality.

⚬

If we are to speak in this fashion about God, we will simply have to use such terms as "within," "under," "at the heart of," and also "beyond," "other than." We may even have to say "up there" and "out there."

The words are faulty. But we have said tiresomely that words are pointers. And surely a thoughtful person can use these terms, understanding that they are not spatial but symbolic in their connotation.

These are the terms that caused Bishop Robinson so much trouble[13]—and apparently many others with him. But just because we say "up" and "out," do we have to have to think in terms of the old, outmoded "three-decker universe"? Surely these words continue to have meaning, even in our incredible universe—and not just spatial meaning, but qualitative, personalistic connotation. However, I don't want to defend these particular prepositions, just the general usability of everyday language.

How else do you express what is known technically as the immanence and transcendence of God? (And we really can't surrender either one.) To say that God is "within" us is not meant spatially but personalistically. But is he not also "beyond" us? We cannot identify God with ourselves—not even all of us added together. So we have to say that God is "other than" ourselves. Indeed, to the extent that he is the ultimate ground and limit of our existence, he is "wholly other"—even while he is "utterly inherent."

[13] *Honest to God,* pp. 11 ff.

There is no avoiding awkwardness of language, no matter how you try to say it. For instance, Robinson writes, "God is not outside us, yet he is profoundly transcendent." [14] Now in the name of clear speech, God certainly *is* outside us. He may indeed be within us. But if he is within you, he certainly is not only within me but also outside me. And even if you add all of us together, if God is the source and sustainer of all being, he certainly is outside us.

God is more than we. He is other than we. Before we were, he is. And after we're gone, he still is.

Language stumbles. But let's not allow our vision or our understanding to fall at the trip of the tongue.

At this point I should like to insert a rather long footnote concerning certain current attempts to remove transcendence from our understanding of God and reduce the meaning of God to immanence. This is frequently done in the name of a Christian approach to contemporary secularism. And I simply want to say that as I see it, to insist that God cannot be in any sense transcendent is to empty the term "God" of any significant content, to render impossible any meaningful talk about God, and certainly to deny any authentic experience of anything more than human. It would be

[14] *Ibid.*, p. 60.

more honest and more convincing to be a forthright humanist.

Robinson has trouble here with what he calls "supranaturalism." He is influenced by Tillich and Bultmann. But what interests me even more is his coy treatment of Feuerbach. Incidentally, Bonhoeffer refers fleetingly to Feuerbach as if with approval. And I would challenge this. If Feuerbach says we no longer have any need for God in religion, the Christian retort is not "Agreed," but "Nonsense!" [15]

So Robinson flirts with Feuerbach, but refuses to go all the way.[16] Robinson seems to want to deny the "supranatural," and seriously limit without completely eliminating the transcendent implications of the word "God." So he sees Feuerbach is a dangerous man to play with because the German philosopher was content to reduce "God" to simply human significance. The bishop recognizes that Nietzsche and Comte issue naturally from such a position. He might also have added that Karl Marx was a convert to at least this aspect of Feuerbach's thought.[17] I'm willing to say that Feuerbach's "essence of Christianity" is really the emptying of Christianity.

A case can be made that this is where any denial of

[15] Cf. *Prisoner for God,* letter of July 16, 1944.
[16] *Honest to God,* pp. 50-51.
[17] Cf. Henri de Lubac, *The Drama of Atheist Humanism,* pp.

transcendence is likely to land us: in a denial of God and ultimately a dehumanization of man. (Feuerbach to Nietzsche and Marx, and their sociological and political successors.)

Van Buren's attempt to express Christian faith in secular terms is surely a fatal bloodletting. By allowing existentialism plus a particular variety of linguistic analysis to deny any transhuman content to the term "God," Van Buren effectively argues that the word no longer has any usefulness. Of course not. But it is a dubious use of words to call this result a secular equivalent of the Christian gospel. It is more like a reduction of the gospel to simple humanism.[18]

A more recent variation on this theme is found in Altizer's *The Gospel of Christian Atheism.* This is the first full-length statement of a position which has been labeled "the death-of-God theology." Actually, "the death of God" is too personalistic a symbol to indicate what Altizer really means. God is not so much a "person" who "dies" as a process which becomes its own opposite. "God" is "a perpetual and forward-moving

---

7-17. I am impressed with the honesty with which French Roman Catholic scholars treat atheism and their insight into its own dynamism.

[18] Van Buren admits this (*The Secular Meaning of the Gospel,* pp. 197-200), but he insists—incredibly enough—that he has left behind "nothing essential" to the Christian faith. A more effective use of linguistic analysis is found in Hordern's *Speaking of God.*

process of self-negation, pure negativity, or kenotic metamorphosis." Personalistic language is really a mystic, mythical symbol for a cosmic process.

And in this process "transcendence becomes immanence." This is what Altizer is getting at when he speaks of "the god who has emptied himself of god in Christ." He denies transcendence. Addressing the secularist, he adopts the secularist's own position. He speaks metaphorically of the death of God, but his intent is clear. "The death of God abolishes transcendence, thereby making possible a new and absolute immanence, an immanence freed of every sign of transcendence." [19]

I can only say that all such attempts to deny the transcendence of God render impossible any meaningful talk about God—and certainly destroy the possibility of any Christian belief in God. We may have to speak more carefully of transcendence than is done in popular religion. I have tried to do this, and have cited the work of some of our ablest young Christian thinkers who are wrestling with this problem. Each of us will have to think this through for himself. Perhaps we can be helped and encouraged by the knowledge that there is a responsible body of thought which affirms that though God is assuredly "within," he is also "beyond" the cosmic process.

[19] *The Gospel of Christian Atheism,* pp. 84, 90, 154.

·•·

Do we need an image? Would a figure of speech help?
Is there some way in which we can picture God as "in,
with, and under" all that is, and yet "other than,"
"beyond" empirical reality?

Interestingly enough—and this is literally true—
only two weeks before trying to write this particular
page I was introduced to a figure of speech which, up
until this moment of writing at least, has proved stimulating.

A colleague who as part of his graduate work is
studying the writings of Charles Hartshorne mentioned
in conversation that Hartshorne has spoken of the
world as "God's body." [20]

At first the image did not impress me. But as I con-
tinued to ponder the reality of God's immanence and
transcendence, the figure turned itself around. And I
began to think of God as "the mind of the universe."
That is, God may be "in" the world as a person's mind
is "in" his body.

This led me to notice a reference in Cobb, who
follows the thought of Whitehead, to whom Hartshorne
stands in close relation. Cobb writes, "The world has

[20] Hartshorne, *Man's Vision of God* (Shoe String Press, 1941),
p. 195; see also pp. 177, 185. Jerald Jackson, who called this to
my attention, has written his dissertation on the subject "An
Investigation of the Implications of Process Philosophy for
Christology" (Northwestern University, 1966).

to God a relation dimly analagous to that of the brain to the living person." [21]

At the very same time I was reading a Catholic theologian and these words leaped out at me: "Just as the human spirit is not identical with the body, but nevertheless expresses itself in the body, so God transcends creation, though this does not minimize the fact that he expresses himself in creation." [22]

Well, now, when two or three hints are gathered together all at once like that, imagination begins to work. That is, ideas are imaged. And because I like to think in distinctively personalistic terms, the images have taken somewhat different forms from the original suggestions.

May we say that the relation of God to the total realm of being is analagous to our relation to our own bodies?

You as a person are immanent within your entire body. You do not try to localize yourself in your body, as if to say the real you is in your brain or your solar plexus. You exist within your entire body.

---

[21] *A Christian Natural Theology,* pp. 239-40. Ogden, of course, takes up this analogy. "I hold with Hartshorne that the interaction between God and the world must be understood analogously to this interaction between our own minds and bodies." (*The Reality of God,* p. 178; also p. 59.) He is careful to add that an analogy indicates differences as well as similarities.

[22] Ansfried Hulsbosch, *God in Creation and Evolution* (Sheed & Ward, 1965), p. 6.

Yet you are not to be identified with your body. You transcend your body. You can say, "This is my body." You command it. You use it. You may even hope to outlive it. In any case, you are more than your body.

I may know your body and never really know you— and this, precisely because the real "you" transcends, is other than, your body.

The analogy is faulty. You are dependent on your body, limited by it, even frustrated by it. Actually, you didn't make your body. It was given to you. For a while, you didn't even know you had it. You had to learn that it belongs to you. But such as it is, it is yours. And not always the most cooperative of instruments.

This would not—or at least need not—be true of God. There are a few differences. He made his own body. Let's not quarrel over the classic phrase, *ex nihilo*. In any case, "the body of God" is utterly dependent upon God for its existence. God indwells it, is immanent throughout it. God may even be limited by it. Still the existence of the cosmos is utterly dependent upon the existence of God. The universe is because God is. But this relationship is not reversible. God is . . . because he is God.

May we suppose that God's relation to the world is like the relation of person to body? Not localized within it, but immanent throughout it? Not identified with it, but transcendent beyond it?

Remember, it's only a figure of speech, a pointer. If it doesn't help, forget it. If it helps, mull it over. Let it prove its usefulness.

REPRISE

Knowing ourselves sustained by an ordered reality and perhaps even kin to this reality, we search for words to identify it. Dare we say "him"?

There is reason to affirm that the deepest reality is Ultimate Person. That in and through all that is, lives and moves a Cosmic Being. He lives and acts purposefully. For he knows that he exists. He knows what he is doing—and why. He is working to the fulfillment of his own divinely held purposes.

Such a Being, though in and through all that exists, is yet more than empirical reality. He is within, but also other than, the cosmos. He is in us, but also beyond us. So we are summoned to meet him as divine Person, to acknowledge our dependence upon him, to accept what he gives us to know of his ordering, purposive will.

4

*H*ow Can We Know God?

*I*f God is a Person, we are confronted with an immediate and fascinating corollary: *Our knowledge of God will be like our knowledge of persons rather than our knowledge of things.* We have said rather insistently that God is not an object among other objects. Therefore, we cannot know God in the same way as we know objects, facts, things, events. God is Person. If we are to know him at all, we must come to know him in somewhat the same way as we know other persons.

From the beginning of this inquiry we have realized that God does not have high visibility in our time. His reality is not readily apparent. We have to look for him. And when we do look, the evidence is not compelling. Even for persons disposed to believe, the reality of God is not always—perhaps not often—easily experienced. This is what is known as the hiddenness of God, and is a most interesting aspect of God's existence to think about.

Several young Christian thinkers have given sharp-eyed attention to this significant fact. They offer varying interpretations of their observations. For our own thinking, these variations may be regarded as supplementary. Taken together, they help us understand the dfficulty in knowing God.

The man who may have been most perceptive in this regard—and who certainly was one of the first to emphasize the relevance of God's hiddenness—sees it as characteristic of transcendence. "The doctrine of the hiddenness of God is an affirmation of the transcendence of God." It is God's way of being "present to man *as* God." [1]

Another young man points out that this hiddenness means that in our knowledge of God, the initiative lies not with us but with him. "It means that God discloses himself at those places and in those ways he chooses and not as man would want." [2] This carries the implication—for still another man—that we may read the disclosing events and processes in alternative ways. There is no clear-cut "correct" reading. "The 'hiddenness' of revelation means that it is always possible to interpret these events as other than a Word of God." [3]

These varying interpretations supplement one another. They all are aspects of our knowledge of God.

[1] Carl Michalson, "The Real Presence of the Hidden God," in *Faith and Ethics,* ed. Ramsey (Harper, 1965), pp. 259, 263.

[2] Harvey Cox, *The Secular City,* p. 258.

[3] William Hordern, *Speaking of God,* p. 123.

The consequence can be very unsettling to the earnest inquirer—even leading to talk of the death of God. "For many of us who call ourselves Christians, therefore, believing in the time of the 'death of God' means that he is there when we do not want him, in ways we do not want him, and he is not there when we do want him." [4]

But I may have run ahead of the argument. I should back up a bit here and ask why it should be this way. Why this hiddenness? As one of my friends says to me, "If God wants to get through to us, why doesn't he just burst in? Why all this lack of clarity?"

It has already been suggested that some of the responsibility may lie with us. And I don't want to relax the tension of that possibility. But there may also be reasons which are implicit in the reality of God himself. These considerations are related to our understanding of God as a Person.

Knowledge as Disclosure

Personal knowledge is of a quite different character from factual knowledge. We usually don't pay much attention to this important consideration. But in order to understand our knowledge of God, we must look carefully at the way in which we come to know one another.

[4] William Hamilton, *The New Essence of Christianity* (Associated Publishers, 1961), p. 65.

It is of the very nature of personality to be "hidden." "The distinctive thing about a person is his ability to hide himself." [5] Things are passive, waiting to be discovered. Persons are hidden, wanting to be disclosed.

To know a person, therefore, is a different process from knowing a bundle of facts. It is true that our knowledge of persons is mediated through facts. We are dependent upon our bodies and their sense equipment to gain information about one another, indeed to know that each other exists. "We never see other persons, only their bodies." [6] But our knowledge *of* one another is different from our knowledge *about* one another.

Each of us, as we mentioned earlier, possesses certain discernible marks: a body, an address, a social security number. We find such knowledge about one another very useful and helpful. (Indeed, the fact that God does not have such tangible characteristics makes knowledge of him rather precarious.) Still, I may know any number of facts about you and not really know you personally. No accumulation of measurable knowledge about you will ever add up to real knowledge of you as person. Something different is involved here, and it is part of the dimension of personal reality. [7]

Who you really are is your own secret and is known

[5] Michalson in *Faith and Ethics*, p. 255.

[6] John Cobb, *A Christian Natural Theology*, p. 239.

[7] Hordern expounds this process of personal knowledge very impressively (*Speaking of God*, esp. pp. 139 ff.).

only to those to whom you choose to disclose yourself. In some instances your self-disclosure is almost involuntary—as when growing up in your family. In most instances it is deliberate—as when you choose your friends. And in a few instances your willingness to disclose yourself may be essential not only to the process of knowledge but also to your personal integrity—as in marriage.

Who you are is your own secret. And you can keep yourself hidden if you choose. But if you want "the real you" to be known, you must be open to others, accessible. To some degree your actions must be transparent so others can "see through you." You must be willing to "give yourself away."

But there is another side to this. If you are to disclose yourself to me in any meaningful sense, I must be open and receptive to you. I must be willing to give something of myself to this relationship. If you sense that I am hard or cold or critical or unsympathetic, you certainly will not disclose anything of profound importance about yourself. If you are to let me know who you really are, I must be open, sensitive, accepting, giving myself to you in the free exchange of personal acquaintance.

You and I could go along for years as business associates, neighbors, or even as friends, without ever really knowing one another. Our relations could be entirely satisfactory and enjoyable on their own level.

There is nothing wrong with such relationships. They are limited, but they may be perfectly adequate for their purposes. Yet if we are ever to enter a relationship of genuine knowledge of one another, we must learn what each is like behind the polite mask he customarily wears. To make such discovery we must be open to the possibility of an experience of quite another dimension. Now there must be trust, acceptance, regard for the interest of the other. Only then can there be genuine knowledge of persons.

Knowledge as Love

Does it occur to you that with complete naturalness we are using words that sound like love? Is it possible that personal knowledge is not so much like scientific investigation as it is like love? Very possible, indeed.

Erich Fromm comments: "The only way of full knowledge lies in the *act* of love: this act transcends thought, it transcends words. It is the daring plunge into the experience of union. However, knowledge in thought, that is psychological knowledge, is a necessary condition for full knowledge in the act of love." [8]

What Fromm is saying is that our knowledge of one another can move to—and, if we desire it, through—various levels. It begins, of course, with the knowledge

[8] *The Art of Loving* (Harper, 1956), p. 31.

gained by the senses: what you look like, where you are, the sound of your voice.

But there is a deeper kind of acquaintance which Fromm calls "psychological knowledge." I see this term as indicating the richer understanding we may gain in further and frank acquaintance. I not only hear your voice, but I learn your opinions and your judgments. I not only see what you look like, but notice how your face lights up at certain experiences, how you laugh and when you frown. I not only know where you are, but what kinds of beauty and interests you surround yourself with in your home. Now I know you more truly than before.

This may even be augmented by psychological knowledge of a technical kind. There might be reason for us to share insights gained by psychological, vocational and aptitude tests. Our knowledge of one another is deepening.

At any one of these points the relationship may level off. We may have reached the point of friendship or acquaintance which is sufficient for our purposes. This is probably where most of us live, most of the time, with most of our friends. But there are some instances in which we will want to go deeper still. And here an element which has been present all along becomes more pressing.

If I am to know you deeply and truly, I must be willing to be known in the same manner. And it must be apparent to both of us that we can be trusted with this knowledge. Here we must be concerned for one another—not only receiving from each other but giving ourselves to one another.

So knowledge becomes love. Love for neighbor, friend, teammate, business associate, husband or wife, child or parent. Each relationship carries its own integrity and requires its own responsibility. To know you genuinely at the level of the relationship that exists between us, I must love you in terms of the responsibility involved. I must be concerned for your good. I must be committed to you as a person. You, knowing this, trust me and disclose yourself to me. And I, in turn, do the same.

Such knowledge is love.

KNOWLEDGE OF GOD

Is this the analogy in terms of which we must understand our knowledge of God? If God is indeed Person, it seems clear that our knowledge of him must be like our knowledge of persons. The image may be limited, as we are limited and as our relations are limited. But our experience—like our words—is a pointer to the divine-human relation which is open to us.

God is a Person. His identity is his own secret. We cannot expect to see his reality plastered all over things like posters on a billboard, nor to hear him announcing his presence like a TV commercial. He must disclose himself in ways which are compatible with his own secret being.

In any case, it is clear that if we are to know him, he must disclose himself. Every theologian I know anything about recognizes that our knowledge of God is utterly dependent on his will to be known. "As Origen once said to Celsus, one cannot seek God and find him without help from God." [9] We can't dig him out if he stays in hiding. Our knowledge depends on his initiative in making that knowledge possible—both by making himself known and by inciting our interest in knowing him.

We may believe that God does will to make himself known.[10] There is no need to suppose that God is either incapable of or unwilling to disclose himself. Rather, it is the whole weight of the Hebrew and Christian belief that God takes the initiative in making himself known. To the best of my recollection, every theologian who has dealt with this issue agrees in some way that the initiative in respect of revelation lies with God, and that God does appear willing to disclose his character and purpose to all men.

Because of the close connection between creation and Creator, some men find evidence of the divine character

[9] Cited by Michalson, *The Hinge of History*, p. 139.
[10] So Cobb says, in Whiteheadian terms, "There does seem to be important evidence of the divine initiative" (*A Christian Natural Theology*, p. 237).

in the realm of nature. "The heavens declare the glory of God." But the language of the heavens is not clear. Nature is at times destructive and apparently cruel. And in any case, the world of objects is not sufficient to reveal the fullness of the Ultimate Person.

Of course "nature" includes man, who serves as an index of a somewhat more indicative sort. But man is a curiously mixed creature, and the evidence is neither clear nor conclusive. Even his religious experiences, which may be given value in this regard,[11] are open to a variety of interpretations.

Moreover, it may be that the divine will to be known must be met by our human willingness to be shown. Perhaps God can't reveal himself to closed, self-contained persons. Maybe we can only read the signs if we are open and receptive. Knowledge of God, then, can never be simply intellectual or analytical. To know God we must be open to the possibility of his presence, trustful of his reality.

May it be that to know God is to love him? How can we love one of whose existence we are not sure? But how can he disclose himself to one who cannot trust him?

It looks as if the initiative really does lie with God. Perhaps this is part of what we mean when we say that God is love. It is of the nature of God to remain open

---

[11] Again, Whitehead was willing to accept the evidence of "religious and moral intuitions"; see Cobb, *A Christian Natural Theology,* pp. 174-75.

toward us, even when we are closed to him. To move toward us, even when we are turned away from him. To solicit our response, even when we are reluctant to notice his presence.

No propositions could prove his reality. No argument could compel our belief. Love must evoke love. And love, to be fully given, must be received.

••

May we imagine one further possibility?

This perfectly personal God, in order to disclose himself to imperfectly personal creatures, may will to appear among them as a person like themselves. This person may be so truly and transparently real that in him is discerned the character and purpose of the ultimately Real.

After all, a person is free to disclose himself at a time and in a manner of his own choosing. You may choose whether or when and in what manner to disclose yourself to me. You choose the words and actions by which you will let others in on the secret of yourself. May we not allow such freedom to God? May not God choose to disclose himself in a particular person, in a particular series of historical events?

We cannot close the argument by reason and say that God either must or did so act. But at least the possibility is raised. And there is another consideration. It just may be that there are limitations in our human situation which require such divine action. If this were true, it would become even more reasonable to suppose that God might be thought to act in such a manner.

Such a disclosure would have to take place under the conditions and limitations of human experience. In order to be comprehensible to us, the person involved would be a person in history, conditioned by his own culture, seen and remembered through the limited faculties of other persons. Yet from the moment of that disclosure, there need never again be any serious doubt about the reality of God or about the character of his being or about his purpose for creation.

Given a God who knows and cares . . . given creatures who are limited and maybe even perverse . . . how shall God communicate to them his reality, his purpose, his caring?

Nature can't carry such such a message. At best, the realm of things and stuff needs an interpreter.

Messengers don't seem to put it across. Seers, prophets, poets, philosophers—their words are not loud and clear.

Maybe a personal breakthrough? A living enactment at the level of man's own comprehension? That is, as a man among men?

REPRISE

The Reality upon which we are finally dependent may be understood as profoundly personal. Indeed, we may dare say that Ultimate Reality is a Person to whom we are called to relate ourselves as persons.

If this is so, he can be known only as persons are known—in mutual self-disclosure, in trust, in love. The initiative, we may believe, is his. Reality not only supports and sustains us, but seeks to evoke our trust, our love. (God is love.)

Such knowledge of God, however, is a decision. It is a choice which we must freely and responsibly make. Just as the natural system of dependable order supports our freedom, so the inconclusive evidence for the reality of God requires our free decision. One might almost think that God maintains this restraint in his self-disclosure precisely in order to keep open the option of faith. Faith is never compelled. It is evoked. To know God—the hidden God—we must choose to believe.

A Funny Thing Happened
An Exercise

A funny thing happened to God on his way to earth . . .

When he got there, nobody recognized him.

Of course, there is a sense in which he had always been there . . .

"He was in the world."

He was implicit in the whole structure of reality . . .

"The world was made through him."

But when he entered the world in this special manner, nobody knew who he was.

"The world knew him not." (John 1:10.)

This wasn't surprising, really.

Who would think of looking for God in a stable . . . or on a cross?

I mean . . .

He looked and sounded and smelled like any other baby.

He grew up to be a rather ordinary looking man,
more troublesome than most, maybe.
And he ended his life like a common criminal.
This is hardly where you would look for God, is it?
Small wonder that "he came to his own home,
and his own people received him not." (John 1:11.)

But . . .
to those who were open to the possibility of his reality,
"To all who received him . . ."
to those who were willing to give themselvs to this
possibility,
"Who believed in his name . . ."
there was given power to become what they knew themselves intended to be.
"He gave power to become children of God."
(John 1:12.)

5

What Shall We Believe About Jesus?

It is obvious that in the previous chapter we have come to a position very close to the biblical view of God. This will be no surprise to some of you. You may have suspected the author's intention all along. And, of course, I have made no secret of my own stance. It is probably true that my personal conviction has shaped and directed the course of the preceding argument. But may it not also be claimed that the steps we have taken have been reasonable, that in each instance there has been good reason for moving in a particular direction? And if we are not surprised when we reach a point so similar to the biblical view, we may still be impressed that the process has been thoughtful.

Transition: Biblical Faith

Biblical faith itself, of course, would never bother with such a procedure. The writers of the Bible are not concerned with philosophical argument. Biblical man

—with only occasional exceptions—does not argue the existence of God. Such a man finds himself unavoidably confronted by a reality he calls God. Biblical man doesn't go looking for God, he bumps into him. (Read the pronouns either way—it is still true.) God is accepted because he can't be avoided. Indeed, man would often like to avoid God, and tries to do so by assorted kinds of disobedience. But there is no dodging Reality.

Such belief is far from wishful thinking or pious comfort. It may indeed be sustaining when life is difficult. But just as often such honest faith is irritating, annoying, uncomfortable. It would often be simpler if God would let us alone. But biblical man knows himself confronted by a God who promises fulfillment and demands obedience.

Such a faith may be deeply devotional, springing from a sense of awe and wonder. Psalm 139 is a classic expression of an awareness of the inescapable presence of God. The most intimate immanence is experienced together with the most awesome transcendence.

> O Lord, thou hast searched me, and known me. . . .
> Whither shall I go from Thy Spirit?

The poet couldn't argue this. He couldn't even understand it.

> Such knowledge is too wonderful for me;
> it is high, I cannot attain unto it.

So he simply confessed it. And his wonder issued in dedication.

Search me ... try me ... lead me.

Or the faith could be prophetic in character, sensitive to God at work in history, shaping the affairs of the nation. So the young statesman conferring with the king gives advice which he believes to be divinely inspired. God is concerned for his people and is willing to be involved in their history. Even the birth of a child may be taken as a sign of the Lord's direction . . . "Call his name Immanuel" (God with us). (Cf. Isa. 7:1-16.)

The very mention of this name carries us into the deeper dimension of New Testament faith, which will now become more openly determinative of our thinking about God. It is not that we must now leave reason behind and appeal only to faith. Reason will still be used, but the guidelines, the hints and indications, will be more clearly biblical.

Once the argument has brought us to a point of contact with biblical faith, we must either draw back or take the plunge. We may conclude that biblical and Christian experience is irrelevant to reasoned discussion about God. Or we may follow the indicators given in biblical faith and see where they lead. The latter is the only course I can follow. So from this point on, though I hope to talk no less reasonably, I shall probably talk like an unabashed Christian.

An "Awkward" Claim

Serious thought about God—in our Western tradition at least—brings us to the question of the significance of Jesus. Christianity has historically made some definite claims in this regard, many of them quite unacceptable to many thoughtful men. Still, they deserve to be looked at carefully.

Christians have been notably consistent on a few points. First, thinkers who otherwise differed widely have agreed on the central significance of Jesus Christ. To be Christian seems to mean, by definition, to take Christ with the utmost seriousness. Who he is and what he does are of primary importance. How this significance shall be stated is, on the other hand, a frequent cause for disagreement. At no point is the language barrier, the sheer limitation of words, more formidable.

Traditionally Christians have agreed at one further point. Here the agreement is not so consistent, but it is notable. It has been asserted that what happened in Jesus Christ cannot be fully explained in human terms. That this life is truly human is clear. That it is simply human is not at all clear. There seem to be unavoidable implications that Christ can only be understood in rela-

tion to a disclosing movement from the direction of
God, a divine initiative that moves toward men.

The centrality of Christ, the uncertainty of language,
and the variety of conclusions are illustrated in a statement of a non-Christian thinker. Some of us would not
want to use the language he uses. But the accuracy of
his judgment is undeniable.

The central question about Christianity concerns Jesus
Christ. If he was God in a sense in which no other man
has been God, then Christianity is right in some important
sense, however Christendom may have failed. To decide
whether Jesus was God in some such unique sense, a philosopher cannot forbear to ask just what this claim might
mean. If, for example, it does not mean that Jesus of
Nazareth knew everything and was all-powerful, it is per-
plexing what is meant. But a large part of what most
Christians mean is surely that Jesus was the best and
wisest man of all time; and many Protestants mean no
more than that.[1]

The awkwardness of language may be illustrated by
a particular discussion in Bishop Pike's recent statement of his own faith concerning Jesus. He admits
that this is indeed the central matter in Christian belief. *The* treasure which Christianity offers is Jesus
Christ himself. Yet Pike insists on the assumption that

[1] Walter Kaufmann, "Faith of a Heretic," *Harper's*, February,
1959, p. 35.

in Christ, God is not acting "specially." Christ must be, he contends, just another instance of God's regular activity.[2]

But why should we arbitrarily assume this? Why should we begin by insisting that God cannot be acting "specially" in Jesus Christ? This is a conclusion at which to arrive, not an assumption with which to begin.

Must we not allow God the freedom to act in a special manner if he chooses to do so? Or if circumstances require it? The only limitation we can place on our conception of the divine activity is that God cannot act in any way inconsistent with his own character. And only to the extent that we know his character can we evaluate claims concerning his action. But what if we can only know his character where he acts definitively, "specially"?

Indeed, it may be argued that we need just such a special action to give us a definitive clue to the character of the actor and an index to his further acts. "In coming to know persons we need 'special revelation.' Certain acts form a 'word' that reveals a person as others do not. . . . The God who is known in all things is not known in any. . . . The believer in special revelation, however, can make meaningful statements about God because he begins from particular events." [3] This

[2] James A. Pike, *What Is This Treasure* (Harper, 1966), pp. 65, 66.
[3] William Hordern, *Speaking of God,* pp. 150, 166. Hordern

special point of reference then becomes the criterion by which to evaluate and understand all the other actions which might be attributed to God.[4]

That Jesus Christ is indeed such a special act of God is the classic Christian claim. It may not be true, and it should be examined. But the assertion seems to be pretty clear.

◆

One way to avoid much of the confusion, of course, would be to settle for what we may loosely call a humanistic interpretation of Jesus. That is, that Jesus was a man just like ourselves who achieved whatever uniqueness, whatever special relation to God we may believe characterized him. This is certainly one of the possible alternatives. As Kaufmann suggested, this is what many Protestants settle for. My own experience amply confirms his judgment.

So a thoughtful layman said to me very earnestly: "It seems to me we're teaching the wrong gospel. Wouldn't it be more convincing and more helpful if we taught that Jesus was a man just like we are? He

---

further claims that "if God is, as the Bible presents him, essentially a person who offers a person-to-person relationship with man, the Biblical form of revelation is the only possible way that God could be known" (p. 164).

[4] Cf. Donald Baillie, *God Was in Christ,* chap. III, esp. pp. 73-74.

achieved a relationship with God which enabled him to become the religious genius he was.

"If he is like we are, this possibility is open to all of us. We may yield ourselves to the divine will as he did, and the few little talents we have can be used much more effectively than they presently are. Just think of the good we could do if all the wonderful powers we have developed were really dedicated to God's will!

"But instead the church goes on teaching that Jesus was divine, or half God and half man. This puts him in a category we can't possibly achieve. We can never follow him, really. So we are frustrated, and may even be given an excuse for failing to achieve."

All this was so well stated and so utterly sincere that I could say only a few things in reply. First, that I respected his faith and the earnestness with which he expressed it. Second, that good as it sounds, this has never been the Christian gospel. (He knows this, and is unconvinced.) Third, that there is something in our human condition that requires more than a human achievement. (He's heard this too, and is not persuaded.)

Why can't we settle for such a humanistic understanding of Jesus?

There are two reasons why this position won't work. The first is that to interpret the significance of Jesus in exclusively human terms simply will not carry the weight which any approximately Christian claim must bear. One can discard the Christian claim entirely, if one chooses—and this is a legitimate decision. But to give any serious attention to Christian faith and experience implies more than simple humanistic terms can convey.

In order to end up with anything resembling the classic Christian faith, certain minimal claims have to be made for Jesus. Van Buren is one scholar who attempts to do this quite without reference to the term "God." He speaks of Jesus as a truly free man who shows us what it means to be genuinely free. Moreover, there is a "contagion" about Jesus; something in his freedom is "catching." So Jesus is "a free man who did not merely challenge men to become free; he set men free." At the same time, it can be said that "whatever can be known concerning 'God' has been answered by the knowledge of Jesus made available in the event of Easter." [5] What Van Buren seems to mean is that we need no longer try to talk about "God." We need refer only to Jesus.

One can only ask how on earth we expect to make such a claim stick. It attributes extraordinary quality to Jesus, gives him unusual status, yet grounds these in personal experience only. There is no reference to "God," because that word doesn't mean anything—or

[5] *The Secular Meaning of the Gospel,* pp. 169, 147.

rather means only human experience. How can we pass this off as an adequate statement of Christian faith? I am forced to agree with Langdon Gilkey that this is a "new linguistic madness." [6]

The basic claims which we must make for Jesus are stated with moderation by Bishop Pike—and still they are considerable. Jesus is "the most." He was called "to fulfill the messianic role [and] accepted it." He was truly human. That is, he was fully open to God. Thus God is revealed "uniquely in the full openness of Jesus." "Jesus was so fully a man; hence what we see in Him is God at His fullest." The most orthodox believer could hardly find fault with these affirmations. He would simply point out that when looked at carefully they still imply that the initiative is from God's side. No matter how full the obedience of Jesus and how essential to the divine disclosure, the "vocation" comes from God. It is God who is able "to break through fully in Him." [7]

A further illustration of the need for careful thought at this point may be found in the wide use of another phrase from Bonhoeffer. It has become popular today to speak of Jesus as "the man for others." [8] This is

[6] The title of his extended review of Van Buren's book in *New Theology, No. 2* (Macmillan, 1965), pp. 39-49. Interestingly enough, the death of God theologians, after eliminating God, give a central place to Jesus. This is a strange phenomenon with little or no visible support in coolly analytical thought.

[7] *What Is This Treasure,* pp. 49, 67, 85.

[8] See John A. T. Robinson, *Honest to God,* chap. 4.

indeed a lovely phrase. But before acclaiming this brilliant insight as definitive, one should read the whole sentence in which the phrase occurs:

God in human form, not, as in other religions, in animal form—the monstrous, chaotic, remote and terrifying—nor yet in abstract form—the absolute, metaphysical, infinite, etc.—nor yet in the Greek divine-human of autonomous man, but man existing for others, and hence the Crucified. A life based on the transcendent.[9]

Now note well. Bonhoeffer does not simply say that Jesus is "the man for others." He also says—indeed, says initially—that Jesus is "God in human form." Both phrases are essential to his thought. It is dishonest to quote him in such a fragmentary manner, using one phrase and not the other. Such editing fails to reflect the wholeness of his thought. Moreover, it is simply insufficient as a way to express classic Christian faith. We must say, with Bonhoeffer, "the man for others." This is splendidly true. But we must also say, "God in human form." Which is just as splendidly—though perhaps less clearly—true. In fact, we can't say the one without the other.

Let me try to say it another way.

There are many thoughtful persons who would like to affirm that Jesus is fully human, that he is the

[9] *Prisoner for God*, "Outline for a Book," p. 179.

ideal man, and let it go at that. But can we let it go at that?

How can we say that this otherwise obscure Jewish teacher who lived in a culture remotely distant from ours is still "ideal man"? How does it happen that Jesus was "fully human"? How does it happen here and not in a hundred other places? Indeed, why doesn't it happen in you or me? How can it be that Jesus was able to empty himself of normal human constraints in order to be fully open to God?

Who can manage this? Just anybody?

Is it possible that only God can be truly human? I would guess so. When we claim for Jesus a special and full humanity, we are also claiming that God has exercised the initiative in this person. We have here a true man because in him God is truly active.

TWO HISTORICAL FACTS

A second deficiency in the humanistic understanding of Jesus is its failure to reckon seriously with the facts of New Testament history. This is admittedly a highly technical field. And the best-equipped scholars differ widely among themselves. So we ordinary inquirers must proceed with caution. However, proceed we must, because Christian faith must square with the facts of history. History does not prove faith, by any means.

But history gives the data for faith. And faith must deal honestly with the facts.

What are the facts?

Let's begin with the simplest: Jesus was a real man, altogether and entirely human. Whether he was particularly unusual is not an issue at the moment. Let's just agree that he was a real, historical figure.

If this seems too elementary, don't rush to conclusions. There have been scholars who have seriously questioned whether Jesus really existed. And there have been others who have said it doesn't matter whether he did or not. For our purposes we may simply note that nowadays it is generally agreed that Jesus did exist, that he was a real person.

However, there is a second historical fact which must be placed alongside the first. We know about this man through documents which were produced in a community that already believed that he was more than a man.

What we have to deal with, then, is not just one fact but two. And the second is just as undeniable as the first. Our knowledge *about* Jesus is gained in documents written by men who believed *in* Jesus. They recounted the human story about this man because they believed him to be more than human. Apparently the only reason we have the account of the historical events is that men already had the faith. The story does not prove the faith. But the two are inseparable in history.

Now how shall we handle these two facts? They present an interesting question for the honest inquirer.

Is there any correspondence between the faith of the Christian community and the facts of Jesus' life? Was there anything in the life of Jesus which elicited the faith of his followers? Is the Christian faith concerning Jesus to be explained as first-century superstition, or as illusion of his followers, or worse? Or was this faith the inevitable explanation of the facts which the followers of Jesus had encountered in their association with him?

Interestingly enough, in answer to this question honest scholars come out at several different points. It might be confusing to indicate what the alternatives are, but I'd like to give it a try. Indeed, we should know what they are so that we can make a reasonably intelligent choice. There are, roughly, three alternatives.

(1) The later faith is a fiction. Let's get back to the simple teachings of Jesus and just eliminate any later teachings about Jesus. (Frankly, this position has little or no standing among New Testament scholars today.)

(2) There is no way of getting behind the faith to the facts. "The historical Jesus" cannot be recovered. We can never know what Jesus actually thought about himself. All we have is the first-century writers' faith about Jesus (Matthew, Mark, etc.). Let's settle for this faith and try to restate it in contemporary terms.

(As I understand them, men as different as Barth and Bultmann take this position.)

(3) It is possible to work carefully in these faith-filled documents—the Gospels, as well as the Letters—and find there some dependable glimpses of the real words and deeds of Jesus. And when we do this, we conclude that the writers' faith is really rooted in the mind and manner of Jesus himself. Jesus said and did things which evoked such faith in his followers. This is the direction taken in "a new quest of the historical Jesus." [10] It is what another scholar means when he speaks of the "implicit Christology" in the dependable accounts of the words and deeds of Jesus.[11] It is expressed in the stark judgment of a German scholar: "The so-called Christ of faith is none other than the historical Jesus." [12]

How shall we choose among these alternatives? I, for one, choose the third. If you prefer the first, you'd better look for other than historical reasons for it. As to the second, it certainly has good standing among

---

[10] Title of a study by James M. Robinson (Allenson, 1959).

[11] So Reginald Fuller, *The Foundations of New Testament Christology* (Scribner's, 1965).

[12] Ernst Fuchs, *Studies of the Historical Jesus* (Allenson, 1964), p. 31. The possible consequences of refusing to regard the New Testament as dependable history are illustrated in Altizer's position. He is willing to suppose that Blake, Hegel, and Nietzsche—not to mention Altizer—know more about the intention of Jesus than Matthew, Mark, and Luke, not to mention John and Paul! This, of course, is an impossible position.

Christian scholars. But so has the third—and it makes the best sense of all to me.

There was something in the deeds and demeanor of Jesus which demanded the faith in him which his followers expressed. His immediate followers came to believe that in their associations with and remembrances of him they were dealing with God himself. God had done something in Jesus that he had never quite managed to do before.

As we examine this first-century faith, we notice a further fact which strikes me as being very significant. In the New Testament there is *no one way* of expressing this faith. The writers of the Gospels and the Letters simply seized the words and images which lay at hand and used them. They made no attempt to correlate and systematize their statements. So there are many and varied figures of speech in the New Testament assertions about Jesus. And nowhere is there any attempt to make all these figures agree with one another. They are there. And they are allowed to stand as they are.

So the Gospel writers quote Jesus as saying, "The Son of man came to seek and to save the lost." "The Son of man also came not to be served but to serve, and to give his life as a ransom for many." (Luke 19: 10; Mark 10:45.) These are authentic words of Jesus, alluding to Old Testament figures. And we must measure their meaning carefully.

The author of the Fourth Gospel expressed his faith

110

in various ways: "The Word became flesh and dwelt among us." "God so loved the world that he gave his only Son." (John 1:14; 3:16.)

Paul reached for other figures of speech: "God was in Christ reconciling the world to himself." "Though he was in the form of God . . . [he] emptied himself." (II Cor. 5:19; Phil. 2:6-7.)

And the entire church joined in the affirmation: "Jesus Christ is Lord."

Frankly, I am willing to stand in this faith. I am willing to let these affirmations say what they have to say. Let them stand as they are. Let's not bother to force them into a pattern of consistency. Let each say what it says.

Then let's try to get at the deepest meaning of these affirmations. First-century images have to be deciphered, translated, restated.

This is difficult. It would be easier to dismiss the whole business as superstition or exaggeration. But that just won't do. We have here a handful of indisputable historical facts. We have here a core of irreducible faith. And to stand with the facts and in the faith is what it means to be Christian.

Where history attests and faith affirms, reason may give assent. What reason has hinted might be possible, faith declares has in fact occurred.

The God who is in and through all that exists has emerged most clearly at one point in history, disclosed himself most crucially in one person. Here we see the character and purpose of God most effectively stated. The divine character and the human embodiment are expressible in one syllable: love.

IMPROVISATIONS

The exposition of this belief can only be hinted at in a chapter such as this. But with the basic theme of the centrality of Christ established, there are several improvisations which might be attempted.

The incognito of Christ. Whenever Christian thinkers speak carefully of God's disclosure of himself in Christ, they always point out that here we are involved—as God is—with both revelation and concealment. What God "says" in Christ is not crystal clear. And how we "read" him is similarly uncertain. So Cox says, "God does not 'appear' in Jesus; He hides himself in the stable of human history." [13] This is dramatically stated, even a little melodramatically. It is more careful to speak of "God's self-disclosure through his self-concealment." [14]

What this suggests is that the ultimate reality of God cannot be fully expressed within the limitations

---

[13] *The Secular City,* p. 258.

[14] Roger Hazelton, *Christ and Ourselves* (Harper, 1965), p. 6. Cf. Baillie, with reference to Barth's doctrine: "His [Jesus's] human life was not a revelation, but a concealment, of God" (*God Was in Christ,* p. 17).

of human reality. God cannot really disclose himself without shattering all the categories of our understanding. And then how shall we comprehend him? If God is to address us in terms which we can grasp, he must limit his self-expression. He must remain partially concealed even in his revelation. And we have difficulty seeing because of our limited vision.

This leaves to one side the whole matter of our deliberate unwillingness to look at what is plainly visible. One dare not dismiss this lightly, but it is another whole subject. It seems sufficient to say now that the limitations under which God chooses to reveal himself mean that he will remain partially concealed. Enough breaks through to give us a dependable clue. But not enough to compel faith.

The uniqueness of Christ. Traditional Christian faith insists that God has done something in Christ that he has not been able to do anywhere else in human history. The disclosure made here is definitive of any other truth about God which may be discovered anywhere else. The deed done here is accomplished once and for all . . . quite literally, "once" and once only; "for all," all time and all mankind.

Many persons, secular and Christian, are offended by this. The doctrine is known technically as "the scandal of particularity," an especially rolling phrase which simply means that to claim something not only special, but unique, about Christ seems like an offense to good sense and to common courtesy. It seems to claim too much for Christianity and allow too little for other religions.

This present discussion must be too cursory to be conclusive. Let me simply say two things.

First, even when we deny the uniqueness of Christ, we frequently assume his uniqueness in a subtle manner. For instance, Bishop Pike says that the reported claim, "No one cometh to the Father but by me," just "won't do." [15] One might reply that such casual handling of scripture will hardly do either. Are we going to eliminate everything we happen to find distasteful? The serious retort, however, is that Pike has already assumed love as the highest value and as the clue to the character of God.[16] And on whose authority, I wonder? Surely, this is a distinctively Christian insight grounded in a certain reliance on Christ's own witness.

Second, I would want to emphasize that the apparent exclusiveness of this Christian claim is inclusive on behalf of all humanity. What God reveals in this person is for the sake of all persons. This instant of time is a moment of truth for all time. What is given here and here only is given for men everywhere. The

[15] *What Is This Treasure,* p. 80.
[16] *Ibid.,* p. 79.

exclusive character of this disclosure is inclusive of all mankind.

The truth about God is given here in a way it is given nowhere else. But once given, it is released for all men. And once known, it becomes the clue to all other truth.

•

The universality of Christ. One of the fascinating conjectures of this Space Age is the possibility of life on other planets. Serious scientists state there is every likelihood that living creatures inhabit other regions of outer space. What does this possibility do to our Christian understanding of Christ?

Surely we may begin by affirming that if there are living creatures on other planets, they are the creatures of the same God about whom we are inquiring in this essay. Moreover, we may agree that these creatures are the objects of his love just as we consider ourselves to be.

This would suggest that God makes himself known to these creatures in somewhat the same way he discloses himself to us. He does for them whatever they require.

We express this faith by saying that the same Christ through whom we know God is the One through whom creatures in any world will know God. Not the same Jesus of Nazareth, mind you. He is the person in human history through whom the eternal God makes himself known to the inhabitants of our earth. This capacity for making himself known is sometimes called "the Word," perhaps "the Christ." And this same Word, this eternal Christ, will constitute God's self-disclosure in other worlds. He will appear there in ways appropriate to the life that is known there. But it will be the same Son, the same Word, the same Christ, who was embodied on our earth in Jesus of Nazareth.

Someone has been quoted as saying, "A one-planet God will no longer do." Actually, we have never had a one-planet God. The New Testament writers, of course, were forced to use figures of speech appropriate to their day. But what they said—translated into the terms of our day—was: Whatever orders of beings may be discovered anywhere in the universe, they are God's creatures; and God's purpose for them will be realized through the same Christ we have come to know in Jesus of Nazareth.

There is a further interesting dimension to this belief in the universality of Christ. There are indications that God's purposes include not only humanity but the whole realm of being. The entire cosmos is to participate in the divine will to redeem his creation. Man may be called upon to respond in a particular way. And consequently man may be called to a particular destiny. But the whole of creation is destined to share in the total fulfillment of God's purposes.

The universality of Christ is not only in reference to all creatures but to all creation.

••

The work of Christ. I hestitate even to mention this subject because it is so grand as to carry us far beyond the limits of this study. But I hesitate even more to overlook it entirely because it is so integral to Christian understanding.

We have hinted occasionally that there seems to be something wrong in the human situation, something off-balance in our posture, something uneasy in our composure before reality. The Christian understanding of man treats this apparent fact with the utmost seriousness. We humans are indeed uneasy, off-balance —desperately so. We are so deeply wrong that we cannot correct our condition all by ourselves. The main difficulty in our knowing God may just prove to be our unwillingness to know him.

God's initiative in Christ, then, is not only for the purpose of the divine self-disclosure, but also for the repair of the human breakdown. In Christ, God not only makes himself known; he also makes it possible for us to know him. And this work affects not only lines of communication with God, but also conditions within ourselves.

The divine initiative is necessary both because of the hiddenness of God and the hurt of man. The divine

117

initiative, then, is not only help to see but health for
seeing. The God who makes, moves in to remake. He
offers not only revelation but also redemption. It is
at precisely this point that the death of God becomes
desperately relevant.

·•·

The suffering of Christ. Here again, at least one
word—even though inadequate—must be said. And this
for two reasons. One is our own experience of suffering, which frequently offers a bewildering barrier to
faith.[17] The second is the clear historical fact that the
life of Jesus was not just a placid, peaceful existence.
He experienced frequent agony and ended his life in a
particularly ungainly form of suffering.

In both instances—our suffering and his—there is
an irrepressible "why?" And the answers are not un-
connected.

We begin with the suffering of Jesus, which we must
affirm is the suffering of God. What happens to Jesus
is caught up into the experience of God. In his concern
for humanity, God suffers. And the divine suffering is
the means to our human recovery.

This gives the context of meaning to our own suffering. If we are committed to God's purpose he will enable

[17] For a more complete discussion of this subject, see my
Even So . . . Believe, chapter 6.

us to use suffering for the greater fulfillment of our lives.

In a deeper sense than I think he intended, Bonhoeffer is right: "Only a suffering God can help." [18] If Jesus Christ is indeed a bodying forth of what God is really like, then we may affirm that we have such a suffering God. God makes himself known to us as the one who suffers with and for us. Therefore we can be helped by him to overcome suffering by the achievement of his will for us.

REPRISE

Reasoned consideration of human experience may lead us toward belief in God. May even lead us to a point where we are open to biblical evidence. Reasoned consideration of this further evidence—all-too-human, indeed, but with a different perspective—may lead us into deeper understanding of God.

The God who, as perfectly creative Person, sustains all of reality is *God for us*. His loving purpose is as dependable as his power. He not only knows that we exist, but he cares. He cares whether we know him and love him.

In order to make possible our knowing and loving him, he discloses himself in Jesus the Christ.

[18] *Prisoner for God*, letter of July 16, 1944.

Here we discover as much of God as we need to know. And because we are given to know God as love, we are called into love of him.

Such knowledge is exactly suited to help us at the point of our free responsibility. God gives himself to us in such a way as not only to sustain, but to restore, our freedom. He not only demands our responsibility but evokes our response. So the responsible freedom which he gives us in order to make us human, and which we compromise in our uneasy self-knowledge, is restored to us to keep us human.

Two Songs

1

He came to us, as if to say,
  I am always with you.
He gave himself, as if to say,
  I am always for you.

But disguised, unknown—
  He was seen
  He was received
Only by those who willed it so.

As then, so now, he is among us
  Disguised, unknown.
His presence waits on our seeing.
His giving waits on our receiving.

Lord, with the gift of thyself,
Grant us grace
  To know thee,
  To receive thee,
Emmanuel, God with us.

2

Do we yet know him?
  "He was in the world,
  And the world was made through him,
  Yet the world knew him not."
How sad, we say, how bad. If we had been there . . .

But
  Like guests at the inn, playing holiday,
  Like soldiers and civil servants, keeping order,
  Like scribes and Pharisees, supporting religion,
We may not know him.

Or
  Like shepherds, believing without certainty,
  Like wise men, giving treasure to hope,
  Like father and mother, all tenderness and wonder,
We may know him.

  For he is given to be received,
  He is disclosed to be discovered,
  He is surrendered to be obeyed.

6

What on Earth Is the Holy Spirit?

*W*e have spoken of God as willing to be known and loved by his human creatures and taking the initiative to make possible such loving knowledge. This implies some sort of relationship between men and God. We need now to ask what this may be. And at no point is the Christian faith more startling and searching than in its affirmation that we human beings may experience a deep and personal relationship with God, the infinite Person.

A RADICAL IMMANENCE

Here is a radical immanence. God is desirous and capable of being personally related to every person who is willing to enter into such a relationship. He does this without losing his transcendence. It is precisely the God who is in, through, and above all, whom we may know and love as a Person intimately present with us. This is a truly radical dimension of the Christian understanding of God.

The word "radical" is subject to varying uses nowadays—and I don't want to add to the variety. But I do want to measure the seriousness of the claim being made. We may be invited to adopt as "radical" a point of view which—on examination—turns out to be a reworking of an old error or a half-truth separated from its better half. What I am proposing is that if we really want to be radical, we should take seriously the classic New Testament faith. Of course, the fact that the proposal is orthodox or sounds "conventional" may mask its startling quality. But I suggest that it is genuinely radical. It gets at the roots of our human experience of God and discloses profundities in the life of God himself.

The Christian faith affirms that the God who creates and sustains all of existence wills to be personally present with those who put themselves at his disposal. His transcendence is never for a moment compromised. All reality depends on his being. But his immanence assumes a radical quality. He wills to be present with us as Person. He can be in personal communication with us. Not just "a bit of God in every man," as conceived in much popular thought. Not a deity defined as the spirit of man or the whole of mankind, an old error currently restyled. But the God who is above all, personally present with every man who will have it so.

This is a radical immanence.

Reaching to the roots of our human experience—perhaps even to the subconscious springs of our behavior.

Revealing a complexity in the divine life which we hardly dare affirm—that God may be more like a family than like a person.

EXPERIENCE AND INTERPRETATION

Such an understanding of God is deeply rooted in New Testament and Christian experience. The doctrine, indeed, is an attempt to account for what had happened. And it may be useful here to rehearse some of these experiences, together with the words which were used to interpret them.

The first followers of Jesus were good Jews who believed in God as creator and sustainer of all that exists, as leader of his people and shaper of their history. With all this in mind they ventured to think of God as Father.

In their association with Jesus his followers came gradually to suspect that he was more than just a prophet or a rabbi. This suspicion became a certainty after the shattering and shaping experience of the Resurrection. They were now convinced that in Jesus they had been confronted in an uncommon manner by the very God whom they knew as Father.

This put a significant strain on their profoundly ingrained monotheism. So they began to look for words to express their faith in Jesus. They found Hebrew terms: Messiah, Son of God, Son of man, Servant. They found Greek terms: Lord, Word. And in the unceasing effort to comprehend and communicate the faith, they used all these words, pouring new content into them, stretching the images into new contours. For this was a new faith.

After the resurrection of Christ, his followers entered into a deeper dimension of experience. They sensed that God was intimately and intensely present with them. They were aware of changes taking place within themselves and they attributed these to the working of God in them. They saw the consequences in their lives, in their relations with other people, and they said it was the result of this inner presence and power of God.

So they took another term familiar to them, the Spirit of God. In the light of their belief concerning Jesus and their further personal experience they changed the word and began to speak of the Holy Spirit. They modified the image and spoke about the Spirit with clearly personalistic connotations.[1]

[1] For the differences between Old Testament and New Testa- meanings see Lindsay Dewar, *The Holy Spirit and Modern Thought* (Harper, 1960), esp. pp. 17, 43. For the personalistic connotations, see pp. 38, 70, 71 ff.

What they were trying to say was that they knew God to be with them personally, profoundly, powerfully. And as they experienced God intimately present in them, they spoke of him as the Holy Spirit.

This New Testament experience was duplicated in succeeding generations. When it came to the first Christians, they didn't pause to think much about it. They were too busy passing the word along. But later generations took time to inquire into the implications of such experience. And so must we. We say that this experience of God tells us something about the being of God. God is so constituted that he is able to relate himself to each of us personally, Person to person.

Once again the importance of personalistic language becomes apparent. And I believe this is one facet of the doctrine of the Holy Spirit. God is not a vast, formless power to be tapped for our use. Impersonal figures of speech will not convey the richness of meaning intended. God is a Person, infinitely capable and equally desirous of knowing us and being known by us personally, capable and desirous of relating himself to us as deeply personal motivation and meaning. This is what we try to say when we speak of God as Holy Spirit.

The inadequacy of words becomes frustrating. Indeed, the imagination falters at this understanding. How can we imagine a God who is capable of relating himself personally to an infinite number of persons? Indeed, imagine one who even wants to do this? Have you ever been in great, crushing crowds of people, looked around you, and wondered suddenly whether God really knows all these people and whether he really cares? How shall we speak of the profound presence of God, intimately known and sensed by anyone who will open himself to God? Talk about a language problem. What words are adequate to carry the weight of meaning involved in such experience?

The term that comes to us out of our history is God as Holy Spirit. It is modest enough—its modesty rendered even more shy by the many connotations which have attached themselves to the term. (What, after all, is Spirit? Or, worse yet, Ghost?) But it seems to be the best word we have to indicate the capacity and concern of God to relate himself deeply to any man who will be open to the divine initiative.

In speaking of God, then, there appear to be three essential truths to be retained.

God as Creator is aware of his existence
    and actively fulfilling his purposes.

God as Redeemer, in pursuit of his good purposes,
    is uniquely present and active in Jesus Christ.

God as Spirit, willing the growth and fulfillment of
his creatures, is personally present with every
person who is receptive to him.

BEYOND PERSONALITY [2]

Do we need a doctrine of the Trinity?

My answer to this question would be "no and yes."
And if you take this as a familiar theological dodge,
let me explain the meaning of such a reply. "No" in
the sense that we do not need a particular doctrine in
which our belief about God must be expressed. There
is no one "correct" dogmatic formula, trinitarian or
otherwise. "Yes" in the sense that we must speak of
God in such a way as to give a basis for understanding
the variety and depth of Christian experience.

"The Doctrine of the Trinity . . . is the effort to discover what must be true of Ultimate Reality because
of what our experience of that Reality tells us." [3] We
must think of God as *being* whatever is necessary to
account for what he is *doing*. Our experience of what
he *does* gives us some indication of what he *is*. We know
him as Creator, Redeemer, Sanctifier (a new term?
Perhaps I had better explain it). Sanctifier is the term

[2] The title of a series of radio talks by C. S. Lewis, later published with the same title (Macmillan, 1945) and subtitled, "First
Steps in the Doctrine of the Trinity."

[3] Henry Pitt Van Dusen, *Spirit, Son and Father* (Scribner's,
1958), p. 151.

referring to God as the one who helps us grow, God as committed to the fulfillment of his purposes in us, God as the one who cleanses, enriches, deepens our lives. And the wealth of Christian experience tells us that the one in whom we believe as Creator is the one whom we know in Jesus Christ, and is the one whom we experience as giving depth and decisiveness to our Christian lives. It is in reflecting upon this manifold experience that we come to think of God as Trinity.

Incidentally, let's be perfectly clear that the authenticity of the experience does not depend on your articulating it in any way. You may know God in all these ways and still have difficulty with any doctrinal explanation of the experience. In fact, experience is always outrunning explanation. But reflection must look back upon what happened and try to understand why and how.

This is why there is no explicit doctrine of the Trinity in the New Testament itself. These documents recount the experiences and their earliest interpretations. But it required considerable reflection, at considerable remove, to formulate a doctrine. In fact, Van Dusen comments that in the development of Christian theology, little attention was paid to the doctrine of the Holy Spirit until the beginning of the fourth century.[4]

Since that time a variety of doctrines has been

[4] *Ibid.,* p. 71.

offered. Each has had relevance to its own time—and some seem to have less relevance than others to our time. Occasionally the church may have been disposed to insist on one way of stating the doctrine as preferable to another. And some ways have been clearly risky, so the church has warned against these. But it may safely be said that modern Protestantism is in no condition to assert that there is any correct trinitarian doctrine. Indeed, some thinkers would be inclined to dismiss the issue as unimportant.

However, we cannot rest easy with oversimplified statements about God. There is a depth and richness of Christian experience which impels us to reflect on the being of God. The experience is what we need: a deep sense of God's personal direction and drive in our lives. Then we will ask what God must be like, the God whom we experience in these manifold ways. Then we will search for words to point toward a Reality which will always be a mystery, but a mystery which seeks to make himself known.

••

There is a further and quite practical significance to the doctrine of the Trinity. To put it directly, thoughtful consideration of what is meant by this doctrine may keep us from running off into assorted kinds of odd—sometimes eccentric—speculations about God. This can be illustrated by three books which are attracting some attention as these pages are being written.

One is *The Christian Agnostic*, by Leslie Weatherhead. The author has a perfectly sound—and really not original—thesis: namely, there are many points at which Christians must be agnostics, that is, admit they don't know. But then Weatherhead indulges in some rather strange speculations of his own. For instance, he is "attracted to the idea that he [Jesus] may be one of a hierarchy of divine beings" who may have achieved deity "either by direct creation and endowment, or by attainment through many incarnations, or by both." (Surely Paul had dealt with such a proposal in his letters to the Colossians and Ephesians.)

Then Weatherhead continues, "From such a hierarchy there may have proceeded other saviors on other planets, all 'Sons of God.'" God may have many such "sons." "God may not be three in one but three million in one." These sons may have done or may be doing on other planets what Jesus did for ours.[5]

A more careful consideration of the doctrine of the Trinity would have saved Weatherhead from such speculations. What the Christian would rather say is that "the Son of God" signifies that divine capacity by which God is able to act in the midst of the historical life of his creatures. We believe he has done this in our history. We believe he can do this wherever

[5] (Abingdon, 1965), pp. 346, 41; see also 183 ff.

it is required and in whatever form it is appropriate. The same Son who acted in our history can act in any history at any point in the universe where there are creatures who need such divine-creaturely action. A forthright doctrine of the Trinity allows for this very adequately.

Two further illustrations of the usefulness of this doctrine center, interestingly enough, in the New Testament idea of *kenosis*, or self-emptying, as Paul applies it to Jesus (Phil. 2:7). The two interpretations are dramatically opposed to each other. And both excesses could be corrected by a more careful weighing of the doctrine of the Trinity.

In an earlier book Bishop Pike had admitted to difficulty with this doctrine.[6] So it is not surprising that when he comes later to deal with his faith in Jesus Christ, he experiences further difficulties. These are evident when he discusses the idea of *kenosis*. Pike interprets this humanistically: Jesus "emptied" himself of conflicting claims, of all distractions, of all self-centered interests, so that he could respond fully and consistently to the divine claim and call.[7]

Now this is a splendid insight and is doubtless true. But it probably is not what Paul intended to say. The rather clear implication of Paul's words is that

[6] James A. Pike, *A Time for Christian Candor* (Harper, 1964), esp. chap. X.

[7] *What Is This Treasure*, pp. 70, 72 ff.

Jesus—or more exactly, Christ Jesus—emptied himself precisely of certain divine status and prerogatives.

I am quick to admit that I cannot quite grasp what Paul is saying. But I think it is decisively more than Bishop Pike seems to allow. And personally I find that a serious grappling with the doctrine of the Trinity helps me to sense what Paul is trying to communicate.

The action moves from God toward us. And in the process there is a sort of "emptying" to which God must subject himself in order to become one among us whom we can comprehend. Then—just as mysterious —this man continues the process of self-emptying: becoming servant . . . obedient unto death . . . even death on a cross.

Oddly enough, a more recent and more extensive use of the idea of *kenosis* falls to the opposite extreme of interpretation. In *The Gospel of Christian Atheism,* Thomas Altizer leans heavily upon this idea. His thesis is that God has fully "emptied" himself into Jesus. So that it now must be said that "God *is* Jesus." [8] (A first-rate heresy, I should think—except that we have discarded the concept of heresy. Let me just say, an impossible statement.) The death of Jesus, then, is really the death of God. And God exists no longer as transcendent being but only as humanity.

Once again it must be urged that this is hardly what

[8] Chap. II, esp. pp. 68-69.

Paul seems to say. It is not that God is totally emptied into Jesus so that "God *is* Jesus." The Christ seems, indeed, to have had a special relation to God—which he surrenders. But God and Jesus are never identified. God honors Jesus for his act of self-emptying; the whole creation will one day salute Jesus as Lord; but all of this will redound to the ultimate glory of "God the Father." (Cf. Phil. 2:9-11.) When all is said and done —as Altizer blithely ignores, or rather denies—there is still God as ultimate, transcendent.

Admittedly we are struggling with words that point to a reality which lies beyond expression. But a serious attempt to understand the doctrine of the Trinity certainly negates any such speculation as Altizer's and makes it possible to sense what Paul is reaching for.

What I am trying to say—at least in part—is that all serious thought about God is difficult. It draws us into mystery, no matter which way we go. And in trying to share this mystery we are driven to the use of words that fall far short of the reality they try to convey. Yet there is a great and historic doctrine which admittedly bristles with difficulties but which is an attempt to say what some men have experienced of God. Difficult as it is, this doctrine of the Trinity is no more difficult than many others which are proposed in its place. And it has additional practical benefits. It will not allow us to draw back into safe but insufficient beliefs about God. And it prevents us from wandering into eccentric and exotic notions which may have little relation to a Christian understanding of God.

·•·

But now it is time for me to suggest what the doctrine of the Trinity has come to mean to me. I do this with great hesitancy. I have no intention of proposing a "correct" doctrine. Indeed, what I shall offer is a minority view among theologians—and I know some of the reasons why.[9] But it is a possible interpretation, and it has proved its plausibility to me.

Let's just try it on for size. If it isn't fitting, you will have to continue your search for a more appropriate image.

I have urged that the personalistic image must be taken seriously in our thinking about God. But I have recognized—and admitted—that such words are only pointers, that the reality of divine personality is beyond anything we experience on the level of human personality. The difficulty lies in finding ways of pointing to this transcendent quality. How shall we indicate what may be "beyond personality"?

That phrase, as I have noted before, is from the writings of C. S. Lewis. It is he who supplied one of the

[9] Georgia Harkness in her helpful discussion of this doctrine takes the somewhat more prevalent view, called modalism: "One God—the only God—comes to us in three vital, indispensable ways" (*The Fellowship of the Holy Spirit* [Abingdon, 1966], p. 116). Cf. the whole of chap. VI.

insights which has stimulated my own thinking.[10] In the little work referred to he notes that we grope for ways of expressing our recognition that God is in some way more than personal. Then he adds that there is one aspect of our experience which suggests what this plus factor may be. It is the experience of two persons in such profound relation to each other that they may be said to be "a union." Each is united to the other in such a way that each is "more of a person" than he would be apart from that union. This, suggests Lewis, is the clue we must follow in our thinking about God. The "beyond" of divine personality is precisely a union of personal beings in an eternal oneness.

Our experience of God suggests a richness in the divine life which this analogy—drawn from our truest relations with one another—confirms: We know God as Father, Son, Spirit. In each instance the relation is deeply personal. We sense that we know God as one God. This analogy allows us to think of him as three Persons eternally related in perfect unity.

Now let me add some further reflections of my own which have been very helpful to me. Let me mention the more recent, less tested one first; then the one that I have lived with longer, which has proved its value in my own thinking.

[10] *Beyond Personality,* esp. chap. 2, "The Three-Personal God."

In our human experience personality does not exist in isolation. A person never exists isolated from other persons. To be a person is to be in relationship to others. Indeed, so far as we know, personality is impossible apart from, and is shaped only in the midst of, interpersonal relationships.

What does this mean for God? If divine personality is indeed perfect, complete personality, this implies that God contains within himself the wealth of interpersonal relationships which constitute the fullness of personal life. God doesn't need the world and he doesn't need human beings to make up for any deficiency in his own existence. He is perfect within himself. That implies that he is not a person-in-isolation, which is an abstraction, really. He is a being of such infinite quality —inconceivably beyond ourselves—that he "enpersons" within his own self all the "interpersonal" qualities of existence.

What does it mean, for example, to say, "God is love"? What is love without a lover and a beloved? This relationship must somehow be realized within the depth of the divine Being.

Maybe I'm naïve. But I have never found it particularly difficult to believe that in the life of God three Persons can exist, inseparably related to one another from all eternity. So that one cannot exist without the others. Each exists only with and for the others. And in the wealth of this perfectly personal existence all the resources required for the fulfillment of the divine purposes are to be found.

Perhaps one reason for this naïveté—if, indeed, that's what it is—lies in a further reflection which has been deeply meaningful to me for many years. I believe we human beings can experience, in a limited way, the manner in which such union of persons can result in a deeper and richer life than is possible apart from the union.

In a good marriage two persons enter into a union in which each becomes more of a person precisely in relation to the other. "The two shall become one." This is not just Old Testament imagery. Nor is it mere sentimentality. It is a profound truth of experience. Two persons can be so authentically open and receptive to each other that they enter into a relation which can only be described as a union. And each is more truly a person because of this relationship with the other.

Admittedly, such a union is imperfect. It is only occasional. It may frequently be interrupted. Indeed, it may be destroyed. But it is nonetheless real. And every well-married person knows it. In fact, many a person, married or not, has experienced this sort of deeply personal relation with another, which has contributed to the fullness of his own being.

The analogy is limited. It is only a pointer to a reality which is quite beyond our human knowledge. But our own experience points toward the divine realization. What we know "in part" is perfectly known in the life of God. "God in three Persons." Inseparably and eternally involved with one another. "Ever one God." This is the language of Christian tradition, enriched by contemporary experience.

How we say it is not finally important. What really matters is that we know God as fully as he offers to make himself known. The Creator whom we trust. The Christ in whom we know the Creator as Savior. The creative Spirit within us, sustaining, guiding, directing our lives.

A simple but eloquent statement of Tillich impresses me as being a fitting conclusion to this section, as it is to his own treatment of this same doctrine.

The doctrine of the Trinity is not closed. It can be neither discarded nor accepted in its traditional form. It must be kept open in order to fulfill its original function— to express in embracing symbols the self-manifestation of the Divine Life to man.[11]

Deep Calleth unto Deep

As reflection on human experience draws us into a deeper pondering of the reality of God, so further understanding of the resources of God leads us into

[11] Paul Tillich, *Systematic Theology, III* (University of Chicago, 1963), 294.

deeper experience of the divine life within us. Doctrine and experience reinforce each other. Experience evokes doctrinal explanation of what has happened. Doctrine suggests the possibility of further experience. At no point is this more true than in our understanding of the Holy Spirit. The work of God the Holy Spirit has special reference to the inner life of men. I should say that the special work of the Holy Spirit is to help us grow toward maturity, help us achieve fulfillment.

Implicit in much that we have been saying in the preceding chapters is a quiet assumption that becomes more firm as our reflection deepens. And now we need to bring this out explicitly.

There is a profound relation between God and man. Man emerges out of a cosmic process. But implicit in that process is the action of God. And when man emerges, the distinctively human qualities of his life are a particular reflection of the life of God. Human personality comes into existence only because divine personality already is. The human person is a reflection of the divine Person. The Bible speaks of this as man's being made in the image of God.

To be human is to bear the divine image. To be human is to be in relation to God. Indeed, the deepest and truest aspect of human existence is precisely this relation to God. This is what makes us men.

Human spirit is close kin to Holy Spirit. This kinship constitutes an indestructible relationship to

God. We humans, by our strange behavior, may deny this relation. We may distort it. But we cannot destroy it. It is constitutive of our humanity. To be human is to be related to God.

It is this profound relationship which makes possible the work of God the Holy Spirit within us. Knowing what we know about God now—since Christ, since further reflection upon Christian experience—we may believe that the Spirit will work in all men to whatever extent he is able. To inspire the search for truth, the love of beauty, the growth toward goodness. Above all, to evoke the experience of love. (After all, we have it on pretty good authority that "he who loves is born of God and knows God." [12]) Everything which contributes to the wholeness of human existence is rooted in the work of God the Spirit. This is what one scholar calls "the natural operations of the Holy Spirit." [13]

However, there is a deeper sense in which we may experience the work of the Spirit. When we come to a knowledge of God through Jesus Christ we are brought into a different and deeper relationship with God. It may even be true to say that we are restored to our proper relationship with God. And it stands to reason that in this new and renewed relation God is able to

[12] I John 4:7.

[13] Lindsay Dewar, *The Holy Spirit and Modern Thought,* pp. 161 ff.

relate himself to us more truly, more effectively, more authentically.[14]

As long as we think of God in ambiguous terms, are uncertain of our relation to him, and selfish in our disinclination to his will, God can work in us only under these restrictions. But when we come to know him as Father, to have an unshakable confidence that we are accepted by him, and to experience an increasing willingness to be open to his will, God is able to relate himself to us more deeply, more effectively.

The reasonableness of such an understanding of Christian experience can be indicated rather simply.

Suppose that you and I are fairly well acquainted with each other, well enough for both of us to realize that you have personal skills and knowledge which would help me to live better than I do—if only you could share those skills with me. You would like to do this. But I am a little suspicious. I'm not sure that you really want to help me. Not sure I can trust you. Not even sure I like you. And under these circumstances there is very little you can do in the way of sharing your skills with me.

But suppose you persist in your openness to me. You really do like me. You put up with a lot of non-

---

[14] I believe this is what Carl Michalson is contending for—in a far more sophisticated and profound manner. See "The Hermeneutics of Holiness in Wesley," in *The Heritage of Christian Thought*, eds. Cushman and Calhoun (Harper, 1965), pp. 127 ff., esp. pp. 131-35.

sense from me. And gradually your attitude begins to soften me up. I begin to trust you. I learn to like you. I have always admitted the value of your skills and wished I might have them too. Now I am open to accept your help.

In this new relationship you can do much more for me than you could formerly. Your openness has opened me. Your steadily proffered love has evoked my love. And soon we both are doing the same things in similar ways.

This is what the church has tried to teach—not always wisely or well—about the Christian life. There have been historic terms for it. Justification is the experience of a renewed relationship with God—a relationship of trust and openness. Sanctification is the term used to identify the continuing experience of growth in personal achievement. It implies a deepening of an inner sense of assurance, a broader sensitivity to others, a wider concern for others.[15]

•••

Modern psychological knowledge helps us to understand the ways of God's working in us. More adequate

[15] Emil Brunner, in classic terms, writes, "Sanctification stands alongside of justification. . . . Sanctification then corresponds to the gradual growth of the new man as it proceeds under the progressive influence of the Holy Spirit" (*Dogmatics,* III [Westminster, 1962], 291).

knowledge of ourselves, indeed, becomes a means of enabling the Spirit to work more effectively in us.

We know today beyond any question that there is one whole aspect of our personal life that goes on at a level too deep for casual observation or manipulation. We call it the unconscious or subconscious—or else, in dislike of the terms, we find other ways of identifying this important range of our life. It is beyond the reach of our immediate awareness. But through various psychological disciplines we have learned a good bit about this region of the self.

We know—all of us have learned this—that much of our motivation wells up out of this deep life of the self. We pay considerable attention to the conscious aspects of our life. These are pretty much under our control. But beyond our beck and call, not subject to our every command, are the deep powers of the self. These thrust up out of their hidden, unknown abode at the core of our being and affect our behavior. These powers may be dark and destructive—and this is what we are most frequently told. But they may also be creative and life-affirming—as the experience of many persons will testify.

Religion deals most often with the conscious life of the individual, the decisions and acts expressive of our responsibility. But what of this dimly known, deeply powerful range of our life? Can God reach us here?

There is reason to believe that God can, indeed,

minister to us at this deepest level of our existence. God as Spirit is profoundly related to the human spirit. We may open ourselves to the deepest penetration and infusion of the divine Spirit into our own being. And precisely here lies the most significant ministry of the Holy Spirit.

It seems to me that this is an area for serious and extensive study. Thus Brunner suggests it is "high time that theology should turn its interest to these psychological realities and powers which have been disclosed to us by depth psychology.[16] Another scholar has discussed at considerable length a "psychological interpretation" of the work of the Holy Spirit.[17] These are only beginnings. There is more to be done—and it would be to the great benefit of all inquiring persons. But it should be done by men better equipped than I. Here I am only suggesting insights that seem to have validity and have been helpful to me.

What is promised is not inexpensive psychiatry, not a quick cure-all for assorted neurotic quirks. What

[16] *Ibid.,* p. 295. Cf. Tillich: "Faith as an act of the total personality is not imaginable without the participation of the unconscious elements in the personality structure" (*Dynamics of Faith* [Harper, 1957], pp. 4-5). And Barth: "The *whole man* right into the inmost regions of the so-called 'unconscious,' is taken in claim" (*Dogmatics in Outline* [Harper, 1959], p. 140).

[17] Dewar, *The Holy Spirit and Modern Thought,* Part IV. He seems to come perilously close to identifying the unconscious and the Spirit; cf. p. 188.

is promised is the opportunity for growth. Growth toward maturity. Growth in love.

This is a process—a process as long as life. And what matters most is not only what we *are,* but also what we are *becoming.* For growth is a constant becoming. Our relationship with God is a continuing process, a movement toward fulfillment. This takes time. But God is patient. He has all the time in the world. What he wants is our assent, our openness, our receptivity. So that his Spirit can be deeply related to our spirit. So that we can grow toward maturity.

This not only takes time, but it takes discipline, practice. The disciplines of the Christian life really constitute another study. They are definable. There have been a good many generations of Christian experience during which men have learned a good deal about personal growth. And the new insights of contemporary psychology are most important.

Practical instruction in the "how" of personal living is very much desired by many people. But it is another subject from our present inquiry. What I want to say here is that such disciplines are well known and may be beneficially practiced. We must keep in mind that disciplines are means by which God is enabled to work in us more effectively, more deeply. He elicits our creative and healing powers as we discipline ourselves to receive and use his power.

147

This takes time. It takes practice. And our son helped me learn this.

In the spring, male fancies take odd turns. Among many there arises the irresistible urge to throw a ball. And I remember early in the life of our son when we first went out in the back yard to "play catch."

The first season was disastrous. He would grab the ball in his fist, swing his arm—and the ball would go in every direction except to me, much to my mounting parental impatience.

The next season wasn't much better. But I learned why. One day I saw clearly that the act of throwing a ball was not only a matter of flicking the wrist or thrusting the arm. As I watched the little fellow struggling with this simple act, I saw that it really isn't simple. His whole body, from the tips of his toes to the tips of his fingers, was involved in throwing a ball. He had to learn how to coordinate his entire body.

No wonder it required several seasons to learn. And now it has become, indeed, a relatively simple act— depending on how serious or precise is one's aim. And the more serious one's aim, the more necessary is practice and discipline.

This experience with my son taught me that the art of Christian living takes time to develop. Indeed, what we have to correlate is not just muscles and sinews and nerve endings. What we have to draw together are conscious intentions and occasional aspirations and conflicting desires and unknown demands—this in the midst of confusing distractions. No wonder it takes time to grow.

And the promise is that God will help us. More deeply than we can know. So profoundly that we will not always be aware of it. Waiting only on our openness—and even inspiring that. Seeking only our receptivity—and even eliciting that.

Is this, then, what the knowledge of God comes to?

> Trust in his dependable sustenance.
> Confidence in his self-giving love.
> Commitment to his evident purposes.
> Openness to his persistent presence.
> Growth toward his intended fulfillment.

REPRISE

The God who has shown himself to be *for* us, wills also to be *with* us. He is infinitely capable and desirous of relating himself to every person who freely opens himself to such a relationship. God wills this as the means of fulfilling his purpose in us, enabling us to become the kind of persons he intends us to be.

The divine capacity to be personally related to us is rooted in the richness and complexity of the very being of God. "God in Three Persons!" Transcendent above and immanent in all that exists. Disclosing himself dramatically and painfully in our history. Intimately and profoundly present with each who will open himself to the Spirit.

And we are built so that we may deeply receive his Spirit. We bear his image. Our person is patterned after his Person. Our spirit, at its deepest level, is kin to his Spirit.

As we, then, accept the loving knowledge of God made possible through Christ, we are drawn by the Spirit into a deeper knowledge which becomes trust, commitment, growth, fulfillment.

*C*oda

What Difference Does It Make?

*T*he pragmatic question is always asked. Does it make any difference what—or whether—we believe?

Well, let's be clear that—as a matter of history—it has made a difference. There seems to be good reason for recognizing that many of the values that are fundamental to our civilization are grounded in the sort of religious belief we have expounded. (Cf., for example, pp. 50-51, above.) Belief in human values seems to be rooted in belief that these values are guaranteed by a divine sanction and are permanent aspects of reality.

It is a very real question whether these values can persist without such grounding in a deeper faith. Some of us would urge that much of our contemporary moral confusion grows out of our very uncertainty concerning the reality of God. So when nontheism is hailed as the liberation of man, we would warn that it is really the destruction of man.

Do we have any reason to suppose that we can build a humane and humanitarian order on the foundation of a humanistic belief? It would be a searching exercise in honesty for a person to ask what happens to human values in a universe that is absolutely empty of divine reality.

The fact is that faith has made a difference. *Does* make a difference. Such an understanding of reality carries with it far-reaching implications for human behavior. The ethical significance of these beliefs is profound and pressing. When we take such faith seriously it begins to shape our lives.

So there is another way in which we may express the difference made by faith. It is personal. It may be unavoidably subjective. But it may be the final answer each man has to give for himself. "This is the difference it makes in my life. And I am confident it can do as much for you."

You may be one to whom this seems unimportant or irrelevant. But let's not assume that you have reached the end of your intellectual pilgrimage. That you have stopped learning. That the issue is finally closed. It may be that something will break open the whole question again. And someone's witness—however subjective— may suddenly be relevant.

The difference made by faith is something which cannot easily be laid out for display. It is the sense of meaning which such faith gives to one's life.

Wishful thinking?

No, I reply. The reflection of reality.

After all, if reality is as Christianity declares it to be, we had better "get with it." If God is, we had better learn to live with this fact. And if God is as Jesus suggests and as Christian experience discovers him to be, we ought to know about it. Then we are ready to hear what men say about the consequences of such faith.

There is a rather consistent body of evidence. Those who take this faith with some seriousness testify with impressive agreement that it gives their life meaning and direction and fulfillment. Subjective words, all— but chosen to indicate the difference this faith makes.

The faith which I have tried to expound in these pages gives *meaning* to my life. There are some who dismiss the necessity for meaning . . . others who continue to search for it . . . still others who seem to ache with its absence. And it is consistently affirmed by those who have chosen this faith that it gives the meaning and purpose which many of us have longed for.

If God is, and if he is approximately as Christian faith declares him to be, the whole cosmic process is given meaning. It all may not be very clear—and some of it not at all clear. But we have confidence that the divine purpose gives meaning to the universe. The dependability of the world speaks of the dependability of God. The irregularities of history reflect the responsible freedom which is an essential aspect of our humanity.

In this context, my own life—though seemingly insignificant in the cosmos—is given meaning. I can never define it exactly. Under God, perhaps, just to *be*. Just to be God's person. That's meaning enough.

Such meaning gives *direction* to my life. (I'm not too good at following directions, but the sense is there.)

What it means to be God's person is never something you can lay your hand on as if to say, "I've got it." It is much more characteristic to say, "It's got me!" This meaning is a process to be entered . . . a venture to be dared . . . a direction in which to be moving.

Here the reality of Jesus the Christ becomes very important. In him I not only find God . . . that is, God finds me. But I also find myself . . . that is, God shows me what I am intended to be. Now I know what it means to be really human.

In him . . . Excuse me, does that phrase bother you? Well, it's a shorthand way of saying, "In the living experience of being found by God through Christ, and thus knowing myself to be God's person." Or, "In the ever-developing relationship with God which is opened up by faith."

"In him," then, I find motivation for wanting to become what I know myself intended to be. Too bad we do such a poor job of being human. Something lacking, somewhere. Courage, maybe? Motivation? Whatever it is, I have found it in this faith.

Here also is guidance. Don't ask how I can be so sure about this. Matter of fact, I'm frequently quite unsure. I test this so-called guidance in every way I know. I frequently worry my way through decisions like anybody else.

But then every once in a while, what the cute coed complained was only silence begins to sound like directions for getting along. What the psychologists portray as a dark, hidden region of my self thrusts up striking shafts of light. Far from infallible, of course. I could tell you many ways in which I mismanage things. My family could tell you more. But there is no denying the sense of direction which this faith has given to my life.

And I have company too. A strange crowd in some ways. Not always attractive. Not always consistent. (We are called "the church.") But basically we are all driven by the same sense of direction.

This meaningful, life-directing faith draws me into an ever-deeper sense of *fulfillment*. This is really living.

This is what I was made for. I tried my hand at re-making myself after my own image—and a botched job it was, too. The hangover from this doesn't exactly help me now as I try to respond to God's intention. And our culture is a strange mixture of help and hindrance. But underneath all the insecurity and awkwardness and downright folly of my life, there is an undeniable sense of fulfillment.

And there's one further word I'd like to add.

There are hints that there may be more to life than we know about at present. This sense of fulfillment which I have tried to tell you about has in it a promise of something more to come. It seems to look beyond history to "eternity." (Another of these troublesome but necessary pointers.) I try not to let this matter too much. But the intimations are certainly present—and ought to be mentioned.

Not that we neglect our immediate history. We have a job to do in the here and now. We're too busy with our present world to be too concerned about another one.

But a hope has been planted. Fulfillment looks beyond history. We don't know much about what that means. And it's wise not to try to know too much. After all, if it's in God's hands, we need not be anxious about it. If we are his, we can trust him—here or there or anywhere, now or then or anytime. For the long hope of eternity is present, giving color and contour to our daily living.

What difference does it make?
All the difference in the world.